THE OBSERVING ONE

AHMED HULUSI

As with all my works, this book is not copyrighted.
As long as it remains faithful to the original,
it may be freely printed, reproduced, published and translated.
For the knowledge of ALLAH, there is no recompense.

THE OBSERVING ONE

AHMED HULUSI

www.ahmedhulusi.org/en/

Translated by ALIYA ATALAY

ABOUT THE COVER

The black background of the front cover represents darkness and ignorance, while the white color of the letters represents light and knowledge.

The image is a Kufi calligraphy of the Word of Unity: *"La ilaha illallah; Muhammad Rasulullah"* which means,

"There is no concept such as 'god', there is only that which is denoted by the name Allah, and **Muhammad (SAW)** is the *Rasul* of this understanding."

The placement of the calligraphy, being on top and above everything else on the page, is a symbolic representation of the predominant importance this understanding holds in the author's life.

The green light, reflecting from the window of the Word of Unity, opens up from the darkness into luminosity to illustrate the light of Allah's *Rasul*. This light is embodied in the book's title through the author's pen and concretized as the color white, to depict the enlightenment the author aims to attain in this field. As the knowledge of Allah's *Rasul* disseminates, those who are able to evaluate this knowledge attain enlightenment, which is represented by the white background of the back cover.

"THEY HAVE NO CHOICE!.."

(Quran 28:68)

"A QUESTION IS HALF OF KNOWLEDGE."

Muhammad (SAW)

"No calamity befalls you on earth (on your physical body and outer world) **or among yourselves** (your inner world) **that has not already been recorded in a book** (formed in the dimension of knowledge) **before We bring it into being! Indeed for Allah, this is easy.**"

"We inform you of this in order that you don't despair over your losses or exult (in pride) over what We have given you, for Allah does not like the boastful and the arrogant!"

(Quran 57:22-23)

TRANSLATOR'S FOREWORD

As exquisitely and descriptively as one may talk about 'What beauty is', ultimately its meaning can be as diverse and numerous as its admirers. Yet no matter how infinitely various its expressions and experience may be, the concept of beauty will always remain **one.**

In a much similar way, although God can be defined in as many different ways as His manifestations, by essence He is One. It is this Oneness, expressed in diverse ways, hence bringing about the seeming multiplicities, that is denoted by the title **The Observing One.**

In other words, the Observing One is the **essence** of all the multitudinous manifestations in the corporeal world, and His infinitely various expressions *is* **His act of observing Himself.**

This act of observing, according to Ahmed Hulusi, is what each individual should strive to experience. That is, to experience God, one must realize the illusionary nature of the constructed self and disable its interference, thereby becoming a conduit of God's interminable acts.

Ahmed Hulusi profoundly deconstructs both the idea of a God up in the heavens, and His representative deities on earth, and urges his readers to embark on an inward quest to discover 'God within'. Compiled mostly of recorded conversations made in 1989, this book is a notable example of the author's ingenious and unconventional construal of classical religious teachings.

Anyone, who has a spiritual yearning and an appetite for mysticism and who at the same time is an unfaltering intellectualist, is bound to enjoy reading this book. Integrating Islamic theology, in particular the esoteric teachings of Sufism, with the findings of modern science, this book enables the reader to **observe the universe within.**

A few important notes:

1. Allah, being the Supreme Name, encompasses all qualities and attributes -both the manifest and the unexpressed- and is used in Ahmed Hulusi's books to denote this reality, rather than *'a god' out there that is separate from the cosmos*. In this light, the word *God* is deliberately avoided and the original name **Allah**, as mentioned in the Quran, is used instead. However, just as it is true for the word 'God', the word 'Allah' also holds predetermined notions of *'an external god'* and this is inescapable for many people. Due to this, the author frequently uses phrases like 'the existence that is **denoted** by the **name Allah**' to draw the readers' attention to the fact that Allah is merely a name **indicating an infinite existence beyond all preconceived and preconditioned ideas.** Thus, it is this existence that the reader is encouraged to contemplate, in reference to the name Allah.

2. Based on the above, **the Names of Allah** referenced throughout the book should not be understood as titles of *'a God'*, but rather as the intrinsic structural qualities of the Essence of existence from which the infinite modalities of the manifest world are derived.

3. Although Allah transcendentally surpasses any gender, the masculine pronoun 'He' is employed not only because using 'It' would be inappropriate and disrespectful, but also because 'He' is the closest realistic translation of the Arabic word *'Hu'*, which has no connotation of gender when used in reference to the Divine.

4. The Arabic word **Rabb**, though generally translated as Lord or Sustainer, is used in its original form, not only because no English counterpart adequately captures its meaning but also the intent, again, is to prevent all kinds of implications to a deity by avoiding excessively used words entailing popularized meanings that are far from the truth.

5. Rasulullah, or **Rasul** is traditionally translated as the *'Messenger of God'*, practically assigning a postman's position to **Muhammad** (saw), who apparently received messages from a physical God in the heavens to convey to humanity(!) Contrary to this primitive understanding, Ahmed Hulusi asserts that Rasulullah is the locus of Allah's knowledge, that is, the focal point of the cosmos through which divine knowledge is expressed and disseminated, **not** a figure in history who walked around preaching to people. For this purpose, it was found more befitting to use the original word **Rasulullah**, or the name Muhammad, instead of the *'Messenger of God'*. (Rasulullah and Muhammad have been used synonymously.)

Twelve years ago, when I first encountered Ahmed Hulusi's books, it never occurred to me that one day I would translate his masterful works into English. I feel privileged to have had this opportunity, and would feel gratified if it aids in a better understanding of the *Observing One*.

Aliya Atalay
Sydney, 2011

PREFACE

Dear Reader,

Composed of the 1989 Antalya conversations, this book presents a unique synthesis of some of the most fundamental concepts of Sufism and the latest scientific findings.

I don't claim to be the first to expound these truths, neither those pertaining to Sufism nor science. I don't doubt that many researchers and enlightened ones have already unearthed and shared such valuable knowledge, though they aren't very widespread and as far as I'm aware a *synthesis* of the two fields has not been done to date.

Those, who have kept up to date with scientific development -not contenting with the knowledge they gained at school - will no doubt appreciate the value of this book. The sections that explain the concept of the **'Holographic Brain and Universe'** and the Sufi reality, based on *the vision of Unity* that **'the worlds are like a dream'**, clearly explicate that science and Sufism arc merely different interpretations of **'the same reality'**.

It is an overwhelming experience of perfection and beauty to witness the **'oneness'**, i.e., the **'reality'**, perceived as intuition or **'revelation'** by those in the past and relayed through allegories and metaphors, arriving at the same truth with scientific findings, now in the 90s!

I had previously stated that 'REALITY', as the Sufis refer to it, is merely a metaphor and these metaphors can be deciphered by everyone to whose lives they are relevant. By all means, the wise reader will understand and experience the knowledge imparted in this book and ultimately, will realize it to be the disclosure of my own understanding.

I penned this book so that those with an interest in Sufism can acquire a general understanding, to serve as a stepping-stone for further studies they may resume through a spiritual master, and as an incitement for the unraveling of mysteries that are undisclosed here.

I also want to take this opportunity to clarify the following:

Twenty-five years ago, when I wrote *Spirit Man Jinn*, I had defined the human 'spirit' as a form of 'MICRO-WAVE' produced by the brain. Anyone, who can recall those days, will appreciate that explaining religion through science wasn't a common practice. In fact, this is why the titular religious had shown so much reaction to my works, making claims such as: *'religion is a matter of faith; it has nothing to do with science'*.

My intention, behind using the word 'micro-wave' to define 'SPIRIT', was not because of the specific meaning of this word in particular, but merely to direct the focus of the reader to the **'realm of waves'** in general. I wanted to indicate that, just like our bodies in this realm, the spirit, being a product of the brain, also has a form in accordance to its dimension of existence, a type of form specific to a dimension of radial origins.

The 25 years that followed gave us an exceptional experience in this field, informing us of the **world of waves** in detail. Consequently, the word 'microwave' began to be used in reference to a very specific frequency of electromagnetic waves, such as those used in today's microwave ovens. As a result, the word I used 25 years ago, to denote something else altogether, became subject to an incorrect interpretation.

Ultimately, I presented a point of view. Those, who feel they are qualified, may complete my work and be more beneficial to humanity.

To elucidate the matter, the word 'SPIRIT' is generally used in the following contexts:

1) To refer to a concrete, perceptible substance that manifests according to **the dimension of its existence.** For example, 'The Realm of the Spirits', 'The Divine Spirit' (*Ruh al-Quds*), 'Human Spirit', 'Vegetative Spirit', 'The Spirit of Earth', 'The Spirit of Hell', 'The Galactic Spirit' and so on. All of these are relevant to the World of Acts (*af'al*) and denote individuality.

2) To refer to an abstract, subjective concept, such as when one claims 'you didn't get the spirit (the point) of it' or 'he has no spirit/soul'… Here the meaning implies 'the essence or meaning of something' rather than it's concrete existence. If I were to say 'he has no spirit' or 'he is spiritless', what I'm really trying to say is that 'he is devoid of spiritual values and consequently of feelings and emotions'.

The word ***Ruhullah*** is also used in this context and has 2 meanings:

a. The manifestation of the attribute of Life.

b. The existence of the meanings denoted by the name Allah.

The verse, 'I have blown into man from MY SPIRIT', means 'I have created humans with the Names and Attributes of my Essence', indicating no concrete or objective substance in any sense, but instead, referring to the Realm of Divine Power (*Jabarut*).

Hence, if we evaluate the word 'Spirit' according to one of the two definitions above, I believe we can attain a better understanding of the context in which it is used.

Based on the above, in this book and future books, I have decided to refer to the spirit of humans, and other beings, as their **astral or radial body** instead of their micro-wave body'. In the future, if I find a better term, I will of course be open to amend it, as what matters more than the word itself is the meaning it denotes.

May Allah protect us from imitation and from being titular believers and enable us to comprehend the 'absolute' realities in the sight of Allah with the foresight of ascertainment.

Amen.

AHMED HULUSI
13. September. 1995
Antalya

CONTENTS

1

REALITY OR A DREAM?

According to **scientific** view;

If we can comprehend the truth, we will understand that a conscious being, who parts from this world, cannot in any way or form come back to continue living an earthly life through another body; simply because, the only permissible movement in the universe is forward.

If we could transgress the boundaries of our biological body and realize a state of radial holographic life... If we could make a leap to the state of pure consciousness and discover our own essence in the Essence of existence... we may finally attain the truth about our former stages, and realize that, in fact, we never actually came into existence in the first place.

How can this be achieved?

Before we answer this very crucial question, let us first consider the following:

While the unequivocal essence of our existence is **consciousness** emanating from **non-existence**, why do we demote ourselves to an unornamented material state, confine ourselves to flesh and bones, and define ourselves as **earthlings**, bound only by earth's course and time?

If I were to ask you 'What is your age?', for example, you might say 'I'm 30 years old'. But is that really so? According to what are you 30? Is this an absolute or a relative figure?

Let us examine this from a **scientific perspective:**

Since your current life is connected to your physical body and your physical body is connected to the earth that you're living on, you are assuming you are 30 years old, based on earth time.

Conforming to this calculation, if you live, say another 30 years, you will leave the earth at the age of 60. But what about after you leave earth, will you continue to think you're 60 years old?

The earth rotates within the orbit and the magnetic field of the sun. This means that every living creature on earth draws its life from solar energy. To put it theologically, we may say that the star called **the sun** is the physical manifestation of **Allah's Attribute of Life** in this universe. Or, rather than **solar energy**, we may call it **'the angelic force which constitutes the sun'.**

All forms of life, on all the heavenly bodies within our solar system, obtain their life and form and continue their existence with this angelic force, within the dimensional depths of the sun.

The brain, which constitutes individual consciousness, evaluates these various dimensions using its sensory receptors and based on these evaluations, it affiliates itself to the field of data that its receptors intromit.

Humans, who embark their journey on earth with biological bodies, continue the subsequent stages of their lives, using the astral-radial body that their biological brains produce during their life on earth.

Since a person who **'tastes death'**[1] becomes detached from their physical body and **progresses to their consequential life in the Realm of the Grave** (*qabir*), or to an independent state of existence in the Intermediate Realm (*Barzakh*) with their astral-radial self, the earth completely ceases to exist in their field of vision. They commence a new form of life within the magnetic field of the earth, orbiting the sun. In other words, they begin living under the

---

[1] Quran, 29:57

administration of the sun and solar energy, hence **becoming subject to the sun's unit of time**, **until doomsday.**

So how long is a galactic year, or one year, according to the sun's unit of time?

As we know, one earth year is the amount of time it takes for the earth to orbit the sun.

One galactic year, then, is the time it takes for the sun to orbit the center of our galaxy, **the Milky Way.** To orbit this point, from approximately 32,000 light years away, **takes 255 million years of earth time.** Therefore, one galactic year is 255 million earth years.

Based on this understanding, a person who dies on earth, at the age of 70, would have **only lived 8.6 seconds according to their real dimension of existence.** When this person disassociates from his biological body at the point of death and enters the Intermediate Realm, the platform of the sun's orbit and energy, he will then realize what seemed to be a 70-year span of lifetime on earth was actually **only a duration of 8.6 seconds!**

This is just like the feeling one gets after waking up from a long **dream** that, in reality, only lasts 50 seconds. Try and remember the last time you had such a dream. Remember how long it felt during the dream and how it felt some time after you woke up. Now try and imagine the relevance of this **'world dream' in terms of the afterlife**, where the sense of time is such that your whole lifetime will feel as if it were no longer than 7 or 8 seconds!

To sum it up, as conscious beings, we are citizens of a much greater dimension of existence and subject to the values and laws of this system. However, our brain's capacity to evaluate this vast field has been hindered by the conditionings arising from our perception that we exist in physical form and thus that we are limited to the 5 senses. Whereas, **'death'** will inevitably wake us up to this truth and force us to realize **the fleeting nature of worldly life.** We will then discern just how short this life really was and just how much our ignorance and inexorable opinions have impeded our potentials.

Let us now try to evaluate the saying of **Muhammad (saw); "People are asleep and will wake up with death"** and the following verses in the light of this truth:

"The Day they see it (their doomsday, their death) **it will be as if they had remained** (in the world) **one evening or half a day."** (Quran 79:46)

"You remained there only a short while, if only you knew!" (Quran 23:114)

Since this world is the 'sowing-field for the hereafter', we can only reap **in the afterlife what we have sowed** in this world, and the total **net** time we have **to sow** our seeds is only 5-6 seconds! If we eliminate the fragile and vulnerable periods of childhood and old age, we really only have a few seconds to **sow our seeds** and **acquire our capital...** a few precious seconds in contrast to the infinite hours of life awaiting us!

If this is the case, let's take a moment to reflect... How much of our time are we squandering on futile things that will give us no return in our future lives, and just how much of it are we using wisely to invest in things that will benefit us in the hereafter?

Now in this light, let's take a look at the source of our judgments, pertaining to our current perception of life, and try to understand this magnificent evaluator: **the brain.**

2

THE HOLOGRAPHIC UNIVERSE OF YOUR MIND

Whether you choose to believe it or not, whether you can comprehend it or not, there is one absolute scientific reality:

You live and dwell within your imagination and your imagination alone!

Electromagnetic waves, transmitted to your brain via all of your senses, are evaluated by your brain's existing platform of data, **creating the multi-dimensional holographic world in which you live.** Regardless of who you are, you do not live or exist in the outside world - you live in an imaginary world that exists inside of your mind.

Any particular thing, that you sense or judge, is no more than your perception of an instance of its existence.

Everyone lives and will continue to live, indefinitely, in his or her own created world. Your heaven and your hell are, and will be, as 'real' as you consider your imaginary world to be real for you right now.

Everything that exists in your world is there based on the values formed by the database of your brain... All, that makes you happy or gives you sorrow, are due to these values in your personal database.

Now, it's the time for renewal!

It is time to discover the existence of our quantum potential; our cosmic electromagnetic awakening; and the multi-dimensional holographic existence created by our wave converter, commonly referred to as the brain!

So let us put an end to all the nonsense about quantum cafes, quantum healing, quantum cakes, and wake up to reality!

But first, let us become cognizant of this:

It is the time to completely reconstruct the teachings that have been imparted to us by **Muhammad (saw)**, the **Quran** and all the saints and enlightened ones, who communicated their message through signs, allegories, and metaphors. It is time to view these teachings in the light of all the scientific facts and resources available to us today.

The most magnificent brain to have ever manifested on earth was the brain of **Muhammad (saw).** He disclosed to humanity the absolute reality. Those, who can comprehend this truth, who have acquired the ability to **'READ'**, will know that the **Quran** is the voice of the Absolute.

Hadhrat Ali, the enlightened ones of late and all mystics have attained awareness of 'the reality' by **'READING'** the system and have explained the same universal truths, but through various symbols and examples that were available to them in their time.

Given the fact that the universal truths have been delivered to us, time and time again, through the use of symbols and metaphors, we too can analyze the topic further by way of an analogy:

Let's assume that a present day modern man, a man that spends his day browsing the internet, communicating globally using internet telephony, aware of all that transpires across the globe in minutes through real-time news flow, was beamed back, 1,000 years in time, to a civilization that does not even have the use or knowledge of electricity. How would such a man explain the tools of our everyday life to those around him? How close to the truth would their perception be? **How could they even begin to understand the actual reality of what is being described to them?**

As such, many enlightened individuals, in the past, have tried to communicate the universal truths to us through the use of symbols, metaphors and examples of their time, to awaken us to the realities that, even now, we haven't completely deciphered today!

Some are able to interpret and grasp the true meaning and essence of these messages, and some, devoid of the capacity to comprehend such knowledge, take these examples literally and fail to understand them.

In that case, the first thing, that we must do, is **to abandon the nonsense that religion and science are two separate things** and reestablish the religious truths, using the language of science!

The system, that science attempts to decipher today, is none other than the system 'READ' by religious individuals in the past, and relayed through various metaphors and analogies. The reality, as described by **Muhammad (saw)**, the Quran and all enlightened souls, is actually the very field of knowledge that science is trying to attain today. Precisely for this reason, in fact, **religious metaphor** should serve as a catalyst in scientific exploration, rather than bringing mythological stories to mind!

If, on the other hand, we devaluate the absolute and universal truth, offered through religion by the postulations of apparent scientific developments void of the essence of religious teachings, we will forever suffer the consequences.

So long as we fail to transform our understanding of religion, based on a God *'up in heaven somewhere'*, into the infinite, universal and absolute truth of **Allah**, we will inevitably live the tragic disappointment of realizing the illusory nature of our assumed reality, as it crumbles away before us!

The only path, to the absolute truth, is to comprehend the reality of **'Allah'** as described by **Muhammad (saw)**, for he neither spoke of a God *'up there'* nor did he suggest *we look for Him anywhere outside of ourselves*! **Muhammad (saw)** is not *the courier or the messenger of a God **out there***! These are outdated and primitive notions! He is **Rasulullah; the locus of Allah's knowledge!**

If you want to explore the teachings of RELIGION, you must do so by looking **within the depths of your 'self', your brain,** the essence of your existence, and not by gazing up into space or observing the sky.

The Quantum Potential... Known in Sufism as **'The Dimension of Names'**, is the infinite potential from which infinite manifestations are birthed. Far from the 'conceptual' world, it is the state in which all concepts, such as time, place, form, and any kind of restriction or limit, are rendered completely obsolete!

The innumerous features and compositional qualities, within this infinite potential, are the designations of the various **Names of Allah.** There are no localized manifestations of Names here, only their potential! This is the state referred in Sufism as the **'Observer who observes His knowledge with His knowledge in His knowledge'** for Allah is *Aleem* (The One who, with the quality of His knowledge, infinitely knows everything in every dimension with all its facets) and this is the dimension of His Infinite Knowledge! One meaning of the verse **"*Alhamdulillahi Rabbil Alameen, ar-Rahman, ar-Rahim*"** i.e. "*Hamd* (observing and evaluating His universal perfection) belongs to the *Rabb* of the worlds (the source of the infinite meanings of the Names) the *Rahman* and *Rahim*" in the opening chapter of the Quran '*al-Fatiha*' is this reality. What the Sufis call **the Unity of Witness** (*Wahdat al-Shuhud*) is also in reference to this dimension.

One cannot speak of **the expression, manifestation**, or **the materialization of this dimension!**

The dimension of Cosmic Electromagnetic expression has been created within, and by, the knowledge of the quantum potential... It is the second imaginary world, and the derivation of all the other dimensions. Its essence is made of the light of illusion. It is an ocean of wave. All that can be, or cannot be, perceived are present as wavelengths in this dimension. The different brain types of different species are the compositional converters of this vast field of waves. The verse, **"*Maliki yawmiddiyn*"** (Sovereign of the Day of Recompense) in the opening chapter (*al-Fatiha*) of the Quran, is in reference to this truth. The **Unity of Existence** (*Wahdat al-Wujud*) of Sufism, pertains to this level of reality.

The brains... The wave-converters of existence! Every individual creates his own holographic world via this converter, and every individual resides within his own holographic world, all the while thinking he is living in an exterior physical dimension. It is this formation that is expounded as of the verse ***"Iyyaka na'budu ve iyyaka nastaiyn"*** (You alone we serve, and from You alone we seek help) from the chapter *al-Fatiha*.

The Spirit... the totality and the point of all 'meaning'. It is the core, the essence, and the 'spirit' of each existence. It also refers to 'life', as each monad of existence is alive, where its life is its knowledge. Indeed, life and knowledge are inseparable attributes! The degree, to which knowledge manifests, is a reflection of the level of consciousness. The 'meaning' and value, of any animate being, is reflected through its spirit. Based on this understanding, we may refer to it as **the expression of the cosmic electromagnetic dimension**, known in Sufism as the Grand Spirit (*Ruh-ul Azam*), the First Intellect (*Aql-i Awwal*) and The Reality of Muhammad (*Haqiqat-i Muhammadiyyah*). Let's keep in mind that these terms do not refer to an object or a person, but to a particular archetypal reality.

Allah... The quantum potential is like a 'point' in respect to the One denoted by the name of **Allah**. One point amongst an infinite amount of others! One point of reflection from within His Absolute Knowledge... The disposition of one world, of one Name, from amidst boundless 'worlds of Names'.

The One who knows His Names with, and through, His Absolute Essence, and 'observes' His Power on His Names! The One who self-discloses and observes His reality, by manifesting His unique attributes through His creation.

The One who created the 'I' and who claims 'I am' through every manifested 'I', yet who at the same time is far beyond any perceiver or perceived!

The One who cannot be contained within any form or perception. With regard to this reality, we can only say: ***"Allahu Akbar"***[2] (Allah is Great).

---

[2] Please refer to the article named *"Akbariyah"* for more information.

In the light of all this, let's now continue the topic on **our universe** and the brain...

It is crucial for us to comprehend that our brain creates the multi-dimensional holographic world in which we live. **But how can we think we exist in an exterior world if, in fact, we're living in the cocoon of our imagination?**

In the first place, what is this dream, within a dream, within a 'dream-like' holographic world and how is it built and structured?

And how does this interior world interact, if at all, with the exterior world?

Each of us plays the role of the 'king' or the 'queen' in our own universe; everyone else is either a figurant or an actor in our play! The roles, we assign to the people in our lives, depend on our 'perception' of who they are, based on our pre-existing database of values. And so we laugh and we cry, we grieve and we rejoice with these imagined figures that we admit into our imagined world!

As we stated above, the brain is a **wave converter...** It receives the infinite waves of **spirit** (meaning) via the five senses and other channels, evaluates and interprets it **according to** its database, then makes a judgment about it and projects his judgment to his imagination! Just like how a TV converts the waves it receives into the images we see on its screen. Hence, from a very young age, we continually construct and reconstruct the multi-dimensional universe in our brain, thinking all the while that we live in an outside world.

It is scientifically evident that what we think we see, hear, smell, taste, and feel, are actually various frequencies of waves that reach our brain and get converted into the specific wavelengths that we define as 'sight' or 'smell' etc, hence forming the multi-dimensional holographic dimension in which the consciousness resides!

In short, each of us live in **our own uniquely imagined world** and will continue to do so indefinitely!

What we perceive and output as 'sight', based on the data we receive from people or objects around us, are no more than an **'instance'** of their existence. Similar to frames of images in a film, our assumed sight is actually based on the data we receive and convert according to our database, of **one still frame**!

Arranging these still images of various instances side by side, we compile albums and albums of photographs and spend our lives flipping through these images!

Upon death, the brain will no longer receive incoming data, as it will be 'plugged out' and disconnected from this dimension of waves. As we move on to our next plane of existence of Afterlife, these albums we've compiled during our earthly lifetime will be the **only provision** we can take with us on our journey. Eventually, **we will commence a new life on a new dimension, and repeat the same process of data conversion using the signals received from the life forms of this dimension as input and our existing albums as database!**

The brain renders the most powerful instances as primary data and creates a kind of *'cache'* memory for quick future access. This is similar to how our computers recall a previously visited page from its cache memory. As such, every time we encounter a previously 'interpreted' thing, whether it be a person, an object or a situation, our brains automatically bring up the most prevalent 'memory' of that thing. Immediately, we begin interpreting and 'judging' and even experiencing certain emotions, all based on some information we stored in the past! This form of preconditioned evaluation is the biggest form of obstruction in one's development.

Muhammad (saw) has cautioned us in this regard with his words:

"If you haven't seen someone for a year, know that the person you see today is not the person you saw a year ago!"

It is for this reason that we must continuously clear our predetermined conditionings - delete our *'cache memory'*- so that we can re-evaluate every situation, according to the current input of data.

The brain, although appearing to be a big chunk of flesh with its neuron-based infrastructure, is actually a mass of frequency that our current level of scientific knowledge cannot yet completely comprehend or decipher. In this respect, we refer to this intricate network of wave as 'THE SPIRIT' and its essence as **'Light'** (*Nur*). *Nur* is knowledge, it is **'data'**. It is like an endless packet of 'meaning' and it is immortal. This is why it is said that **"we shall taste death"**, and not 'cease to exist'!

Let's remember that the person, across from us, is also living in his/her own cocoon world, or in other words, their individual multi-dimensional holographic universe. When our brain converts the data waves of instances relating to his physical existence, he takes his place in our holographic world and we think such and such person 'exists'! But the fact is, we 'define' his existence, his character, his role and even his effect in our lives!

This is why the great Sufi masters referred to this life as a 'dream', and in reference to it said, "We come alone, we live alone and we die alone".

Some of us are confined in a cocoon (multidimensional holographic world) resembling a castle, while some of us live in slums; some of us decorate our homes (brains) with precious collections, while others fill it with garbage. Some of us don't even have a home and are referred to as 'homeless' (or 'brainless' in slang.)

Our holographic universe is the world that we are going to live in for eternity. How we interpret the instances of data waves we receive, who and what we admit into our world and where we place them is either going to create our heaven, or our hell.

The instances of data waves, that reach our minds, will be evaluated and based either on the 'garbage' that we have already brought into our homes, or based on the new homes we construct with the guidance of the universal system '*Sunnatullah*'[3]. The world, the intermediate realm, resurrection, heaven and hell, are all experienced within, and are all shaped by our personal interpretations and evaluations.

Upon death, after the brain 'shuts down' and ceases to function in its 'flesh' form, a 'system reboot' will occur and our life will

---

[3] *Sunnatullah* means the laws and order of Allah, i.e. the mechanics of the system, the laws that govern the manifested worlds.

continue to run with the back-up of our astral (wave) brain. Thus, we see the importance of backing it up with solid and functional knowledge!

Everything, described in **the Quran** and by **Muhammad (saw)**, is reality and *will* be lived! The important thing is to decipher the meaning of these verses correctly, without misconstruing them or taking them *literally*. For instance, **Muhammad (saw)** says that **man will be resurrected (recreated) from his coccyx (tailbone) in the afterlife.** To construe this as a physical resurrection of the body made of flesh and bone is nothing but ignorance. Clearly, this is a metaphor to suggest that a 'form of life' will continue after death. Or for example, he says **"the sun will come within a mile of the earth"**. This corresponds with today's scientific understanding that eventually **the sun will engulf the earth, and the earth will be vaporized.**

Muslims have even misunderstood the verse regarding the 'spirit'. When **Jewish scholars** enquired about the **spirit** to **Muhammad (saw)**, a verse was revealed in answer to their query, telling them **"Little has been disclosed to you about the spirit"**. This verse is addressing the Jewish scholars, telling *them* that 'little or no knowledge', regarding the spirit, was given to the *Jews*. Indeed, there is a significant amount of information regarding the spirit in Islam, whereby **Ghazali** states,

> *"One, devoid of the knowledge of the spirit, cannot reach enlightenment."*

Our spirit is our very existence! It is our world. **Muhammad (saw)** says:

"Your spirit is your body and your body is your spirit."

We are what we perceive!

However...

We also contain within us the potential of **vicegerency** (caliphate), to which we have become ignorant! **We have become unaware of this gateway that opens to the dimension of our cosmic electromagnetic expansion!**

If we shape and fill our world with the wealth that awaits us behind the gate of vicegerency (the properties of the dimension of Names!), then our worlds will transform into paradise and eventually we will unite with Allah. The following verse refers to the purification of one's world, i.e. one's perception!

"The purified and the refined will be emancipated" (Quran 87:14)

We weave our cocoon world, not only with the genetic information we inherit but also with all the conditionings that we receive throughout our life. Our database is 'based' completely on these preconditioned values, channeling and shaping our lives, for better or for worse!

In short, our lives are based solely on externality. We are never truly aware that our lives are spent within a cocoon that we weave ourselves, and not in an outside world!

Although we experience a sample of our **cocoon-like existence** each night when we go to sleep, we don't recognize or conceive it! In the state of sleeping, we are all alone, neither our partner, who may be lying right next to us, nor our children, in the next room, nor anyone else are with us!

When we experience death and move on to a non-material state of existence, all instantaneous impressions are left behind, including people and objects. We travel on alone in our journey, taking only our conditionings and perceptions with us.

In the past, prophets, saints and enlightened people have used symbolic and metaphoric language –due to the lack of scientific knowledge- to share the universal truths with people and to wake them up to the reality of their cocoon-like world.

The goal is to cleanse our minds from predetermined judgments, based on data waves of instances, and to renovate our holographic worlds with substantial material, in such a way that it becomes transformed from a slum house, or a hoard house, to a palace befitting a sultan.

A sultan is one who lives in correspondence with the Names of Allah, a vicegerent!

One, who can break out of his cocoon, will be emancipated and promoted to the dimension of cosmic electromagnetic expansion as a friend of Allah (*waliyy*), where his world will be 'paradise-like'.

Muhammad (saw) says:

"In paradise, each person will possess a whole world of their own, the smallest of these will be 10 times bigger than earth, and they will be told: 'Wish what you may, for all your wishes will be granted!'"

In other words, each person will be the sultan of his or her own world.

As for those who have chosen to live in slums, i.e. those who did not develop their brains but chose to fill it with garbage instead will forever suffer its consequence!

Either use your brain and research and evaluate the truth scientifically or surrender to the path drawn out for you by **Muhammad (saw)** – for there is no other salvation.

3

DATA STORAGE IN THE BRAIN

The brain's perpetual process of storing memories and information begins at birth and continues until death.

Various types of data reach the brain in the form of waves. By programming the receptor cells according to their own frequency, the data take over the activities of these cells, imposing their own informational content upon the brain. Whether we call this conditioning, or programming the brain with specific information, it makes no difference, as the effect remains the same.

The brain, by its nature, is designed to receive and accept all forms of information. When a child touches a hot stove for example, and we yell out "No! Hot!", we inadvertently condition the child's brain, so that the next time a hot stove is encountered, the child will automatically define it as 'hot!..'

As such, in time and with experience, certain judgments are dictated to the brain, leading us to acquiesce in the false belief that we are composed of a 'physical body'. Henceforth, based on all the different information we store in our brain we begin constructing a **'standard of judgment'**, which stays with us until death. Unless that is, we become informed of a better alternative with which to replace this information.

All this informing and conditioning then leads us to the belief that the administration of our body belongs to us. Consequently, we perceive ourselves as a separate physical body, and this idea that we are an 'individual unit', separate from the 'whole', becomes our biggest obstruction. As a result of this conditioning, we become punished with a lifestyle that is deprived of the 'Universal Essence' in our origin.

But how about the superfluous conditionings, to which we are constantly exposed, from our environment? Indeed, our environment presents us with all kinds of information, but it doesn't enforce it upon us.

The mechanics of the System does not tolerate excuses.

It is 'us' who have the final say as to the information that we want to absorb. It is up to 'us' to observe, study, inspect the data presented, check it against our latest attained knowledge and verify it. We must examine the data in accordance with scientific findings, determine whether it is correct or not, then make a decision to take it or leave it, rather than blindly accepting everything we are given.

Metaphorically speaking, accepting any given information, without conscious observation, is like burying our lively consciousness into the lifeless grave of the body, oblivious of how 'free' we may seemingly be. **One, who cannot escape the grave of the body while living, cannot escape the grave of the earth after death!**

The inability of the individual consciousness to recognize the grave-like nature of a life, that's confined to the conditionings of the physical plane, will inevitably result in the imprisonment of both the body and the soul. If the Afterlife is the consequence of our life now, then **the failure to escape the prison of our bodies**, during our life here, will yield a continued state of imprisonment in the Realm of the Grave (*qabir*) after death, trapping us both within the confinements of our ego, and the physical grave.

Then, our first and main priority must be 'to consciously grasp the truth of our existence!'

Who are we really? What are we? How are we?

Evidently, our existence is not indistinguishable from our physical body; we cannot perform the simplest of tasks without the use of our bodily functions. If we don't nourish our body, then our brain, which is sustained by the activities and the input of the body, cannot execute the myriad of functions for which it is designed.

Furthermore, the **astral body** called the **'spirit'**, with which we continue our life after death, receives all its input and consciousness from the brain. Thus, it is crucial that we provide the brain with exactly what it needs. Being both the creator and the mediator of the spirit, the **brain** uploads its own properties to the body it operates, enriching the body with its own qualities. As such, it is imperative that we provide the brain with its due right, **without blocking our conscious and without becoming entrapped by the desires of the body**. Failure to implement this will impede our self-development and thus render us prone to unfathomable damage.

Only when we lose our physical body, and see what it feels like to exist purely as **consciousness**, will we conceive to which point we have impoverished ourselves. But alas, it will be too late, for we would have relinquished the chance to compensate for our losses.

Therefore, it is of paramount importance to understand the body, its true function, the spirit and its purpose. Who exactly is the **'I'**, contained in our 'soul', carrying within it the **'Essence'** of our existence? What precisely is consciousness? What are its qualities?

A genuine apprehension of these realities will enable us to adopt them into our lifestyle. It will upgrade our quality of life here, and also warrant us the ensuing consequence. Whereas, subsisting in negligence would lead only to deprivation.

As stated in the Quran:

> **"Whoever does an atom's weight of good will see it, and whoever does an atom's weight of evil will see it."** (Quran 99:7-8)

> **"And never will you find in The System** (course) **of Allah** (Sunnatullah) **any change."** (Quran 48:23)

Everyone, in accordance to the regulations and the criteria of this System, is either going to perform or fail to perform the necessary deeds for their emancipation. Excuses are futile.

Rasulullah [The manifestation of Allah's knowledge] advised us of the deeds that will yield benefits for us, and warned us of the actions for which we will face repercussions.

These teachings have been offered to us, **not by enforcement**, but **by advice, caution, and invitation.**

4

HIGHER MATTER

Until now, I've attempted to explain our inadequate evaluation of the **actual structure of the universe, due to the limited nature of our sensory perception[4].**

Time and time again, we've explored the sequence of 'sub-matter', breaking matter down to the level of the cells, atoms and subatomic particles, until finally reaching the level of pure energy.

However, we never really directed our attention to **'higher matter'**, that is, the opposite extreme of the sequence; going from matter, up to a 'higher state' of matter.

When I say **'higher matter'**, I don't mean **another form of matter that is somehow higher than our current one.** As stated before, matter as we know it, is only an assumed reality, **based on** the interpretation of our senses. This being the case, there is also **a higher dimension** of this projection!

Let's try and understand this, by way of an example:

The human body is composed of trillions of cells, which we can view with the aid of specialized microscopes. In reality, we're far

---

[4] This topic has also has been thoroughly covered in my books *Universal Mysteries, Spirit Man Jinn, Muhammad's Allah* and *What Did Muhammad Read?*

from having completely deciphered all of the functionalities of the cells in our body.

What exactly are all these cells doing? What kind of relations do they have with one another? How do they live, and how do they die? How are new cells generated?

For the most part, we live our lives completely unaware of all this.

Each of the cells, in our body, maintains their life and functionality based on their unique structural properties. In actuality, trillions of cells in our body have all proliferated from one primary cell! The genes contained in the chromosomes of this primary cell, carry all of the information necessary to synthesize every other cell to accomplish all of the tasks during one's lifetime. In other words, our kidneys, liver, brain, heart and all other organs are nothing but different molecular compositions of these cells. Despite having completely different functions, all of our organs come from the same source! And **each one of them possesses their own unique consciousness, mission, and mechanism.**

Now, when we view a body from outside, we say **'a human body'** and see it as one 'whole' structure. We don't see all the different cells composing the body. We don't evaluate the countless chemical activities that are constantly taking place from the view of our organs, or more accurately, the cells that constitute them. We simply view them as a 'mass' and roughly label them as 'the lungs', 'the heart', and 'the kidneys' and so on...

A similar situation resonates on the levels of **higher matter.**

If we allegorize our galaxy, composed of approximately four hundred billion stars, as a human body, the stars can be likened to the cells or organs in a body.

Just as the liver possesses its own unique structure, processor, organic consciousness, and a mission that it attempts to accomplish with these means, so too the stars, which are like the cells or organs in the gigantic galactic body, are endowed with a conscious level of life.

When earth is viewed from space, neither plants, nor animals nor any humans can be seen. Earth appears merely to be a separate 'mass' of matter. It is however, inhabited by humans, animals, plants and other species, that are all equipped with unique properties and further sub-divided within themselves accordingly.

In the same way, the galactic structure can also be viewed as an individual body, an entity with a personality! This galactic structure, that we call **'The Milky way'**, is actually **a living unit, a life form**, only perceived as such by another galactic structure, not by us.

Just as humanity has consciousness, so does the earth. The structure that we refer to as the 'earth' also possesses consciousness that is specific to it.

Just as the earth has consciousness, so does the sun, and just as the sun is conscious, so is our galaxy!

The consciousness of the sun, in comparison to the galactic consciousness, is like the consciousness of a single cell in our body, in contrast to our consciousness. Our galaxy subsists in the universe as a conscious individual being, amongst millions of other such galaxies!

The constellations, that are associated to the zodiacal signs, are also conscious cosmic beings with unique characters. **Muhyiddin ibn al-Arabi** refers to these cosmic beings in his **Meccan Revelations** *(Futuhat al-Makkiyya)* as **'the angels residing in the 12 constellations'**. When we state that there are billions of galaxies in the cosmos, what we're actually saying is that there are billions of conscious entities within the galactic realms of the cosmos!

So, if the similitude of the sun, in respect to the galaxy, is like a single cell in respect to our whole body, then to even try and comprehend the place of the earth, let alone an individual living on earth, is almost impossible!

Indeed, to expound the place of a human being in respect to a star, or a star in respect to the galactic body in which it dwells, is quite a challenge. We have always put our limited senses to work in the exploration of **'sub-matter'** and pursued the path to the microcosm, without really evaluating **'supra-matter'** and the macrocosm.

How could we have? This is like trying to view the human body from the nucleus, or from a chromosome within the nucleus of a cell! How can a single gene, on a chromosome within the nucleus of a single cell, have a complete view of the body it inhabits? Clearly, this is not possible. It can't even **see** or **comprehend** a single organ in the body! The cytoplasm, surrounding the nucleus in which it lives, would seem like an infinite ocean to this gene!

Based on this then, it is senseless to say that *the space between a particular planet and a star is empty, or void.*

As mentioned before, everything is composed of atoms, and, the atoms that make up my body are no different to the atoms in another object. As such, all of us are an interconnected part of a composite compound. In other words, **at the level of atoms, we are all 'one'.**

It is this reality of **'oneness'** that invalidates the **'empty space'** between the stars. **From the realm of the atoms to the galactic dimensions**, the 'unity' of our existence abolishes all concepts of division and emptiness.

Our eyes *perceive* the stars to be randomly scattered in space, separate from one another by so many light years... Whereas in reality, the stars are no more apart from one another than the individual cells in our body are to each other. On the contrary, the apparent **'emptiness'** in space is 'satiety!'

Whether it is our lack of knowledge, or the limitation of our senses, we fail to recognize, and duly evaluate, the galactic body and its consciousness.

Based on the reciprocal truth in the Hermetic maxim, 'As above, so below', it is not inappropriate to say that the 'ego' and the awareness, possessed by each of us, is also inherent in the galactic being of which we are a part, even though we may not be aware of it.

The place that we occupy in the universe is like the brink of the membrane surrounding the Milky Way in our local group of galaxies. There are approximately 30 galaxies in our locality. That is, 30 **'conscious galactic beings'**, perhaps **a family of them!**

This being the case, we can't even be likened to a single cell in the body of 'one' of these galactic beings! If we suppose that our

Solar system is like a single cell, you and I are but one person amongst the billions of people residing on only one of the heavenly bodies in this solar system!

One form of the beings, referenced by the word **'angels'** in religious terminology, is this **'Spirit' within the galactic dimensions**; i.e., a galactic consciousness...

Indeed, a mystic who tried to expound on this grand Spirit once said:

> *"We have discovered an angel so great, that it is not even aware of our existence!"*

Just like a single cell in our body may not necessarily be aware of the structure we call 'the brain', or our brain may not be aware of a particular cell that comes to life, or that it grows and proliferates, then dies in some part of our body...

Every cosmic dimension is perceived as **'matter'**, according to the receptor senses of its inhabitants. This is similar to how we perceive the objects, in our dreams, **to be of the material world...**

If we take the scale of existence to be like a ruler of infinite length, and assume the level of pure energy to be at zero point, then the quarks, ions, atoms, molecules, cells and what we perceive to be material objects can all be placed in the range between 0-50 cm. So, if the material realm in which we are living, and everything we perceive to be 'matter', is within this range, and beyond the point of 50 cm, there are infinite forms of life within the universal dimensions of the macrocosm.

How infinitesimally small is our place in the universe!

The evaluation of **the infinite nature** of such existence is unfathomable for us. Nevertheless, with a little straining of our intellectual muscles, there will be great value in the understanding that we can attain as a result.

As an extension of earth and our life here, **the Afterlife**, and the dimensions we refer to as **Heaven** and **Hell**, are all parts, perhaps organs, of the aforementioned galactic body.

This grand, glorious and magnificent being is only one out of billions of others, and part of a 30 member tribe or family residing on this side of the universe, encompassing our galaxy…

What are they talking about? What are they arguing over? What are they thinking? We live our lives completely unaware of all of this.

A cell in a human body is like the Solar system in the Galaxy!

Is everyone completely oblivious to this reality?

No!

This is the pivotal point!

No matter how small or big the primary structure, whether it's the microcosm with all its genes, bacteria, muons and quarks, or the macrocosm, encompassing the sun, the stars and all the heavenly bodies and galactic beings…

All of their 'essence', in terms of the Absolute Essence (*dhat*) and according to 'holographic reality', is composed of the same 'substance'. Hence, any form of life, regardless of its position on the scale of existence, can establish a form of communication, an interaction with all of the units of life within the infinite micro and macro realms in the cosmos.

Provided, of course, that they journey within and discover their own essence first. As this form of communication is based on the principles of the **Absolute Essence** (*dhat*), one who hasn't connected, to the 'Essence' inwardly, cannot correlate in the network, outwardly.

Primarily, we must free our consciousness and escape the blockage caused by the imposed limitations of our realm of existence. All of the conditionings, judgments, emotions, and fragmented perceptions have to go! Our consciousness must be cleansed!

For we know that the cosmos is a manifestation of the Knowledge of the Infinite and **the Absolute One.** As such, **the Absolute Essence and Knowledge, the Divine One** is present in every particle of existence!

Thus, **the essence of your consciousness**, the **'Essence'** of your being, is no different to the essence of an atom or a galactic entity in the micro or macro cosmos.

However, because our **consciousness** has been subject to, and formed by, bodily conditions, it has been hindered by various assumptions and postulations. As a result, it has become a molded and obstructed **'separate conscious'**, detached from the universal reality of 'Oneness'.

Whereas, 'consciousness' is not even a tangible thing with a certain form or mass. One does not incorrectly condition the consciousness by pricking and poking at it, but **conditions it by imposing and uploading fallacious information to it.**

Our consciousness can be purified, from such misinformation, according to the intensity of the communication that can be established [from the realm of The Absolute Essence (*dhat*)] **with the micro and macro beings in the cosmos.**

Evidently, many mystics and saints are known to have established such forms of communication. Indeed, anyone, who is able to break out from the **'cocoon'** of their sense perception, can access the infinite network of the universe.

The biggest veil, that conceals our consciousness, is the **'veil of words'**. Words, or labels, and the images we've linked to them in our minds, blind us from attaining a tre understanding of the reality.

By identifying with the images we've linked to certain words in our minds, and believing them to be true, we stop seeking for more, and hence, prevent ourselves from seeing the absolute reality.

Consequently, our worlds become smaller and smaller.

Our whole lives become centered on basic needs and wants.

We become consumed by the things we eat, drink, buy and own and become confined in the base and primitive states of matter.

Our only reality becomes the material world and its corporeal affairs.

As mentioned before, the time, that we have to spend in this apparent material world, is so transitory in contrast to the life awaiting us.

The inhabitants of the macro dimensions are very grand and varied, though we have collectively labeled them all as 'angels'. In actuality, they are all beings of the planes of higher consciousness.

If we don't recognize this truth now, we will not have the opportunity to do so in the future.

Just as there is no impertinent component in our bodies, every organism has its unique mission and functionality. Just as the astral body, within our physical body, possesses its own consciousness and mission, there also exists, in the macro plan, conscious beings with unique missions.

If the sun takes 255 million years to orbit the Milky Way, then the sun is only 8 years old since it has only completed 8 tours around the Milky Way in its entire course of life.

Since we are 32,000 light years away from the center, or the 'heart' of that Galactic being, we're nothing more than an electron in one of the cells somewhere on this galactic surface, of which there are billions of others!

Like us, they too come to life, grow, and die, and like us, they don't become **'nonexistent'** with death, for death is but a change of dimensions for conscious beings.

When viewed in this light, how futile it seems to rejoice over something gained, or feel sorrow for a loss in this world. Just as nothing we earn or possess, in a dream, has any value when we wake up, none of our worldly possessions are going to be valid in the afterlife. If we don't want death to wake us up from a bountiful dream world to a desolate reality, we must wake ourselves up from our denial now, and start building our real world on the foundations of real knowledge.

When we are dreaming, all sorts of things happen to our bodies. We get shot, hit, perhaps even deformed, but we always wake up to find our bodies completely unblemished and intact. Moreover, our sense of **'I'** or **'ego'** never ceases to exist.

The **'I'** is ever present throughout our dreaming, regardless of what occurs to our apparent bodies. This is because the body, in our dreams, is of a spiritual nature, and since the spirit isn't composed of parts, it doesn't get fragmented.

Different laws govern different realms of existence. As such, the Afterlife also has its own set of administrative laws and conditions. **Nevertheless, our sense of 'I' will never be lessened, regardless of how we live, or whatever pleasure or pain we experience, our consciousness and spirit will feel each and every bit of it.**

What will be the capacity of our spirit and self-consciousness?

The degree, to which we develop them in this world, until the point of death, will be our fixed capacity indefinitely, in the Afterlife! What we fail to recognize in this dimension of existence, we will never have the opportunity to recognize in the next…

If we don't strengthen our spiritual body now, we won't get a chance to return to this dimension, to compensate for it later.

What we can't comprehend or fathom now, we can never comprehend in the future.

We are not just the macro of the microcosm, but also the micro of the macrocosm.

Muhammad (saw) says:

> **"There are some angels, who have attained the State of Certainty** *(Yaqeen)* **who are not even aware of the existence of either this world or humans."**

In the same way, we are not aware of the cells that are constantly coming to life, growing, serving, and dying in our bodies.

If we don't expand our consciousness and enlarge our comprehension now, if we don't get to **know ourselves** in terms of the 'Absolute Essence' and connect with the system and attain the universal realities while in this world, we will never have the opportunity to do so again. This is because; death will replace our worldly endowments and capabilities with those qualities that are more befitting the nature and conditions of the subsequent dimensions.

"And whoever is blind in this [life] **will be blind in the Hereafter…"** (Quran 17:72)

Undoubtedly, the **blindness**, mentioned in this verse, is not in reference to a physical condition, but rather to **spiritual blindness**, or, the incapacity to recognize and evaluate the reality. The only way to be enlightened, from this kind of darkness, is by absolving our consciousness from unnecessary and false information.

Muhammad (saw) says:

"The state, in which you live, will determine the state in which you will die. The state, in which you change dimensions, is the state you will continue your existence indefinitely, in the Afterlife."

To summarize:

We seem to occupy an intermediary position in the universe, right between the micro and macro worlds. Mankind is the transition point between the states of energy that comprise un-manifested matter and the 'supra' states of matter.

Every dimension is inhabited by specific entities, receptor systems to evaluate these entities, and a perception of matter based on these evaluations.

The cell, and its perceptible reality, as opposed to the reality perceived by an atom…

The corporeal world, created by our brains, as opposed to the ethereal world of the celestial galactic beings… And so on.

In terms of their origin and essence, the **consciousness**, that is present in all of them, stems from **One Source: The Spirit.**

In Sufism, the identity of The Spirit is referred to as The **Perfect Man** *(Al-Insan Al-Kamil)*, and its consciousness as The **First Intellect** *(Aql-i Awwal).*

How imperative it is, that we understand our place and structure within the infinite micro and macro worlds. How crucial it is, for us to achieve this understanding to avoid dying like the billions who pass away without conquering themselves… Those who were able to see the truth will look at those who couldn't and say **"another one has passed away"**, like a leaf falling off a branch, our departure will mean nothing for the universe.

So let's stop wasting our time and energy on things from which we are inevitably going to part. Let's start living with the awareness that our possessions, our loved ones, and all of our worldly accumulations are going to stay behind, when we continue our journey on to the next dimension.

Let's accrue more of that which will enlighten our journey ahead; let's increase our **knowledge**, elevate our consciousness and raise the frequency of our vibrational energy.

Now that we have become aware of the higher states of matter, or The **Angelic Realm** (*Malakut*), let's now explore the Realm of **Divine Power** (*Jabarut.*)

In the following chapters, **'The Observation of the Essence'** and **'The Discretion of the One'**, I will try and elucidate how the **Absolute Essence** (*dhat*) evaluates existence with the attribute of Knowledge, once our consciousness is purified and our souls are refined.

5

THE OBSERVATION OF THE ESSENCE

"Has there not been over man a period of time, when he was not a thing worth mentioning?" (Quran 76:1)

"I was a hidden treasure and I loved to be known, so I created heaven and earth. I created Adam so that I may be known."

"Allah existed and nothing else existed with Him. And He is now as he ever was."

"Allah created Adam in His own image, or, in the image of *Rahman* (the quantum potential from which everything obtains its existence)."

"Where was Allah before He created the heavens and the earth? He was in Absolute potentiality (*Ama*) above and below of which there was no air."

What are these encrypted messages telling us?

Be it the verses of the Quran or the sayings of **Muhammad (saw)**, evaluating these timeless truths, according to the knowledge and understanding of our current time, will provide us with invaluable insight and enlightenment.

However, the primary prerequisite for such enlightenment is the removal of the thick veil of the 5 senses. For, without freeing ourselves from the conditionings of this blinding veil and its illusory world, we cannot see the truth for what it is.

Nonetheless, the cocoon-like reality, spun by our sensory perceptions, or the 5 senses, is not altogether purposeless. It actually renders a crucial function in one's primary growth. Like a mother's womb, it aids in the cardinal development by nurturing and preparing us for the real world. Hence, it is not designed to be a perpetual abode, rather a temporary sheath of protection during our development. Just like a matured baby pushes itself out of the womb, or a developed silk worm breaks out of its cocoon, the matured consciousness must also hatch out of its **cocoon-like reality**, lest he suffocates and withers away.

Our biological bodies and this worldly life are like our cocoons, designed specifically for us to develop and enhance our Afterlife skills, so that we can survive and thrive in the hereafter.

If our consciousness fails to break through this cocoon of the 5 senses, it will never attain the truth about itself. As a result, we will always be subject to the stimulations of our rigid sense perceptions, i.e., the physiological and chemical stimulations of our body will shape our reality, in which we will eventually suffocate.

The 5 senses renders perhaps one millionth of the brain's capacity of performance. It has been given to us as a sample (trial version) of the brain's infinite specifications and qualities.

The human brain shares a similar process of development with countless other life forms on our planet. That is, the brain is formed by molecules, which are formed by atoms, which are nothing more than clusters of energy.

When I say energy, I'm not referring to the static or kinetic forms of energy that we study at school. I mean the energy that is the source of life of the whole of creation.

The genetic structure of the DNA and RNA molecules, contained in each and every cell of our bodies, is subject to undergo mutation if exposed to certain cosmic radiations. Modern science can modify and manipulate the genetic configuration in laboratory settings, exposing these molecules to certain waves and radiations and creating other species as a result.

Interestingly, X-rays have been found to have the same effect on the **neurons** in our **brains.**

Our **consciousness** is the '**I**' that develops on the database of our genetic and astrological data, synthesized with our acquired environmental conditionings. In reality, our consciousness doesn't belong to the physical body; it is a by-product of the brain's exceptionally comprehensive activities of analysis and synthesis. It pertains to the soul!

Though the universe is satiated with infinite forms of life, each form is recognized only by those who share the same dimension, and who have the capacity to perceive and evaluate them.

That is to say; first, the sensory perception is formed, then the material world is perceived. Or, first, the radial analyzers are formed, and then the radial world is perceived and evaluated. **The expressions and their meanings rely on the life forms that perceive and analyze their wavelengths.**

Now let us remember an imperative truth:

There is no existence other than the infinite and boundless *Uluhiyya*[5] **named 'ALLAH'.**

Since there is no limit to Allah, it is impossible to think of anything that is 'other' than His Being.

In one aspect, this infinite boundless Being is *Al-Jami*, gathering all the expressions unto Himself. In another aspect, this Being is *Al-Muhit*, embracing and encompassing the whole of existence. Hence, the expressions, that are contained in Himself, are **contemplated in His Knowledge, again by Himself.**

---

[5] *Uluhiyya* is the entirety of the manifestations of Allah's Names throughout all dimensions.

There are no other beings in His Being, for no other being has come into existence other than His Being.

"He begets not.

Nor was He begotten." (Quran 112:3)

No other existence other than His existence can be thought of.

"Only Allah exists, and nothing else exists with him. He is now as He ever was."

'Now' is the 'now' mentioned in this verse. Concepts of time, place, matter, space, etc., are only valid **according to the 5 senses.** In this dimension, however, time is the consistency of the 'now'. In other words, time is nonexistent, outside the dimension of our perception.

If only we can surpass the barrier of our physical eyes and start basing our lives on scientific and spiritual truths... Perhaps then, we will realize that this world is composed of innumerable forms of life, ranging within **wavelengths** of a billionth of a centimeter to kilometers of length, **each with unique expressions and significance.** This animated world is the **World of Acts** (*af'al*).

Each of these layers of expressions contains specific meanings that are perceivable by certain other expressions. They become labeled as the **'unknown'** (*ghayb*) and hence remain concealed only to those who can't perceive them. This isn't an **'absolute unknown'** however, only a **relative unknown.**

To the extent we become conscious of our own essence and escape the limitations of the 5 senses, we can decipher and observe these **unknowns.**

This observation will not be ours however; it will be the observation of the Absolute Being.

The Observing One!

The observation of the **now**, as there is no other time other than this very moment now.

Only those with a purified consciousness can live this reality.

"He wanted to observe the infinite expressions contained in Himself, hence He shaped His creation such that they contain His expressions."

Where?

In His infinite Knowledge!

It is crucial to have a correct understanding of these words and their meanings. Creation is the form of His expressions that He wanted to observe.

When I say **'form'**, I don't mean physical form, but **the form of 'meanings'**, as He is *al-Musawwir, the fashioner* of infinite forms derived from the implicit realm of meanings.

When contemplating on this, we shouldn't let our minds run through images of earth and the billions of people residing on it.

Just one galaxy in our universe can contain up to millions of suns, let alone billions of other galaxies that haven't even been discovered yet. Whether we think of the macrocosm out there, or the microcosm within, there is no space that is void of meaning.

It is in this light that we should evaluate the phrase:

> **"Has there not been over man a period of time, when he was not a thing worth mentioning?"** (Quran 76:1)

That time is now. Not some time ago in history.

That is, right this very moment, there are such grand and magnificent dimensions, so immense and extensive, that amidst these, humans are not even worth mentioning! That is, except for those who have elevated their consciousness and ascended to higher realms. So, if we don't want to be amongst those who aren't worth being mentioned, who have no significance in the universe, then we must realign our way of thinking.

Let's remember what **Muhammad (saw)** said:

> **"Do not curse time *(dahr)*[6], for time is Allah."**

---

[6] *"Dahr"* refers to eternal time as opposed to the time of our physical dimension.

Time *(dahr)* is an infinite, limitless moment!

When Allah wishes to observe an expression of His Names, He merely wills for them to manifest.

"Verily, when He wills a thing, His Command is, 'be' (*Kun*), and it is!" (Quran 36:82)

That is, His very thought of a thing is the act of manifesting that thing. The minute it's thought of, it's already done.

There are no such concepts like the past and the future for Allah!

Whatever meaning He wishes to manifest, he shapes an appropriate form in an appropriate dimension, and experiences that meaning through that form.

Where?

Not within, nor without.

The emanation of a form, and the experience of a particular meaning, occurs through the revelation of the inherent meanings of the form.

Hence, the meanings and conditions, that become explicit through the form, are what compose the form in the first place. The form's experience of its meaning is the result of the environment, conditions, and events that cause it to be.

All of this is created **within the Knowledge** of the One.

Actually, all seemingly animate and inanimate beings are nothing more than names in the realm of His Knowledge.

Their apparent **presence** is only of **a hypothetical nature**, based on being **'acknowledged'** in His Knowledge.

In other words, existence is a trust given unto us. The illusion, that we exist outside of Allah, is due to certain names or labels that we are given.

Like assigning a label 'x', to a hypothetical data in an algorithm. It doesn't have a substantial existence of its own, but because we say 'x' we assume x exists, whereas in reality it is only a hypothetical figure.

In actual reality, only Allah exists.

According to whom?

According to He who observes his creation through the eyes of those who have 'conquered' (*fath*) their true essence, by attaining the **High Station of Sainthood** (*Wilayat-i Kubra*) at the consciousness level of **The Pleasing Self** (*Nafs-i Mardhiyya*).

Thus, all 'things', that we affirm to be existent, are nothing more than the forms of His Names created in His Knowledge. **Things don't exist independently.**

When evaluated from the Realm of Knowledge, everything that supposedly exists, according to our senses, turns out to be nothing more than **'forms of knowledge'.**

To put it simply, **the whole of creation is a composition of Names.** All of the innumerable and various dimensions in the cosmos are different compositions of His Names.

Those who reach the level of **The Pure Self** (*Nafs-i Safiyya*) are those who are able to break through the conditionings imposed by the explicit 'forms' on the implicit meanings.

They are those who abandon their hypothetical existence and dive into the ocean of **'nothingness'** and become **'everything'.**

Through realizing and living their **'nothingness'**, they attain the level of **'Oneness of Being'** (*Wahid'ul Ahad*), hence becoming everything!

Now let's try and understand the following:

> **"Each will act in accordance to his creation program** (*fitrah* - natural disposition).**"** (Quran 17:84)

That is to say, whatever purpose, individuals are created to fulfill, the means to achieve this purpose will be made easy and attainable to them. The decisions and actions, that are necessary for the execution of their mission, will be made attractive and pleasant, such that they manifest what is in their nature with ease.

"Your *Rabb* (reality of the Names comprising your essence) creates and chooses as He pleases, they have no choice (or say) **in the matter."** (Quran 28:68)

As can be seen, if you are meant to be bound by conditions, restrictions, and not break out of your cocoon, then the act of hatching your cocoon-like reality will be made difficult for you.

That being said, the act of breaking out, or leaving the womb, whether it is an animal giving birth or some bug trying to hatch its cocoon, is always **a difficult process!**

It follows then; the act of breaking one's cocoon-world of 'matter' to reach the boundless Angelic Realm (*Malakut*) of the heavens should not be a simple process...

As with any transition from one dimension to another, the transition is an **'awakening'** (*ba'th*) that is, a new birth, a new beginning, a 'first' after a 'last'...

But for some, this process is made relatively easy or attractive... because Allah wills it so...

An incalculable, limitless structure! Layers of 'meanings' beyond comprehension! A 'name' that points to His existence, but which isn't conditioned or even completely defined by it!

You, I, and it... We all exist as different expressions of different compositions of His Names... But to experience 'existence' as a whole, without fragmenting it, requires the abandoning of the 'you' and the 'me'.

Only once we become **'selfless'** can we become **'one'**. And only once we become 'one' can we attain and live true **'love'.**

The 'self' is like a curtain between the lover and the beloved, when the lover annihilates himself in his beloved, the curtain will be lifted, 'duality' will disappear, and only love will remain.

When one 'likes', one wants to possess. But when one 'loves', he loses his 'self' in his beloved. He abandons his identity completely and becomes nullified in the beloved. This micro experience of **UNITY** then gets rippled out into the cosmos, transforming it into a macro experience of **Unity**, until 'individual' consciousness perception and experience, becomes completely obsolete.

Let yourself abandon your 'you' and let me abandon my 'me' so that we may meet in 'nothingness', and be!

According to one narration:

What begins at the 'point' ends at the '*alif*[7]'.

That is, everything begins at the point of **'Oneness'** (*Ahadiyyah*) and ends at the '*alif* of **'Unity'** (*Wahidiyyah*). The whole of existence is only one reflection, referred in Sufism as the 'One Theophany' or the **Divine Self-disclosure of Allah** (*Tajalli Wahid*).

According to another narration:

What begins at the 'point' ends at the '*sīn*[8]'.

Where *sīn* indicates **'human'** in Arabic, and the point is the 'One' (*Ahad*).

The Quran begins with the letter '*bā*'[9] of the '*basmalah*[10]', or to be more precise, the point beneath the *bā*. When this point is extended it becomes an *alif*!

Just like when one wants to draw a line, one begins at a 'point' which then becomes the source, from which the line extends. The '*bā*' of the '*basmalah*' is the source point of all of the characters in the Quran. The point never changes. Every character is a series of points that come together and seem like lines. In their essence, they are repetitions of the same point!

Hadhrat Ali says: **"I am the point beneath the *bā*"**, perhaps to mean, **"I am none, yet I am all... I am the '*alif*".**

---

[7] Alif (ا) is the first letter of the Arabic alphabet, and represents unity depicted by its single stroke.
[8] Sīn (س) is the 12th letter of the Arabic alphabet. As a word 'sīn' is synonymous with 'man' or 'human.'
[9] 'Bā' (ب) is the second letter of the Arabic alphabet, and the first letter of the Quran. It holds a symbolic value in Hadhrat Ali's acclaimed saying "I am the point beneath the bā", the point referring to individual experience being the result of their intrinsic reality.
[10] The *Basmalah* is an Arabic noun used to refer to the Quranic phrase "*b-ismi-Allah-er-Rahman-er-Rahim*" found in the beginning of every chapter of the Quran, which literally means "In the name of Allah who is Rahman and Rahim."

The last chapter of the Quran is called **Nâs**, which means **humans.** As mentioned, the letter *sīn* is representative of a single **human.** Hence, the chapter '*Yasīn*' means '**O humans**' (or 'O mankind').

Eventually what we have is a semi-circle, going from the '**point**' to '**man**', and the journey of man back to the point.

Uniting with Allah, in essence, comes about, in man, **with the knowledge of the 'point'.**

Will the knowledge of the point make mankind (*nâs*) obsolete?

Since, in terms of their actual reality, humans do not have an independent **existence**; it makes no sense to talk about losing something that doesn't exist in the first place.

It was mentioned above that **He manifested as creation, the 'meanings' He wanted to observe.**

We were told these meanings were **99** in total, albeit this figure is only in reference to the 'samples' and not the whole. Just as our 5 senses give us some insight into the innumerable qualities of the brain, the 99 Names give us an idea about the infinite meanings encompassed by the **One** (*Ahad*). Evidently, an infinite and unrestricted being will possess infinite and unrestricted meanings.

In consideration of this endless, limitless truth, how devastating a loss it is - to indefinitely confine oneself to a tiny little cocoon world based on the 5 senses and the fleeting, temporal, local bodily desires.

"O mankind! Whilst I have created you for myself, with what are you busying yourself? On what are you spending your time?"

Who is this verse addressing?

Those who have the innate capacity to hear the message... Not those addressed in:

"They are like cattle-nay (*an'am*), they are even less conscious of the right way: it is they, they who are the [truly] heedless!" (Quran 7:179)

To be a mirror to the One from whom we derive our existence, essence and origin, or, for the One to reflect on our mirror, we must first be cleansed from the contaminations and conditions of our illusory humanly being.

As Jesus says:

"You are not thinking God's thoughts but human thoughts."[11]

If we observe our essence from a 'material' human perspective, and live our lives like an iceberg in the ocean, then surely we can't reflect Him duly.

The world and everything in it are like games and pastime for humans...

The whole of existence has been desired, designed and shaped for the observation of **the Reality of Muhammad** (*Haqiqat-i Muhammadiyyah*) and **The First Intellect** (*Aql-i Awwal*).

If you have been created to be one of the 'observers' of meanings, then escaping from the 5 senses and humanly emotions and conditionings will be made easy for you. The process of cleansing your mirror from emotions, thoughts, conditions, bodily and subconscious desires that can obscure the Reflection, and reaching your essence will be simplified for you.

Nevertheless, just as some grains become wheat and bread and eventually make their way to our dinner table; many others are lost in the field and don't amount to anything.

To love **Muhammad (saw)** is to be like Him, to acquire His knowledge and consciousness, to annihilate one's self in Him.

One cannot taste the honey from its jar.

To love is to become the beloved.

Eventually all things will fulfill their nature and return to their essence, hence actualizing their innate servitude to Allah.

"All animate and inanimate things are in service to Allah."

---

[11] Matthew 16:23

"Humans and jinn have been created to serve Allah."

All of these mean one thing: for whatever purpose you have been created, you will fulfill it one way or another. Life, conditions, skills you have been given, all of these will inevitably channel you to perform your innate worship, i.e., manifest your true essence, whatever that may be.

Our final destination will either be to get sloshed and agitated in the **World of Acts** (*Af'al*), or to freely swim in the realms of **His infinite Names** (*Asma*), or to manifest and observe the qualities of **His Essence** (*Dhat*), or else to realize our **nothingness** and become nothing in His infinite, **boundless Being.**

However one lives one's life, that is how one will die, and however one dies, that is how one will live in the Afterlife.

The frequency, at which our brains function just before the point of death, will be the last bit of information uploaded to the spirit that our brains render. Hence, when the spirit becomes detached from the brain, it will continue functioning at the frequency with which it was last uploaded.

Therefore, if at the point of death, our consciousness level happens to be functioning at a low frequency, conditioned by the 5 senses, and consumed with worldly and bodily desires, and then we will have to live the consequences of this state in the Hereafter.

If, on the other hand, our consciousness happens to be vibrating at higher frequencies, freed from sensual conditionings, we would have attained the level of the Observers of the Truth, watching and observing the infinite bounty of His Names expressing themselves in ever unique and incredible ways upon creation. That is, the level of **'loving the creation, due to the Creator'!**

These are the people about whom the general public says: "such and such lives on another plane... He walks, sits, eats and drinks like us, but he isn't like us! Who knows where he is right now?"

He would be swimming in the ocean of meanings in the dimension of consciousness... He would be wondering in the dimension of Allah's Names.

Some people who reach this state become veiled to what goes on in the corporeal world, while others experience both dimensions simultaneously. This state is commonly referred to as the **Contented Self** (*Nafs-i mutmainna*) and the **Pleased Self** (*Nafs-i Radhiyya*) and it is the state one attains as one becomes cognizant of the reality of his soul.

The consciousness will wonder amidst these meanings in the realm of **Reflection of Names** (*Tajalli Asma*) knowing that they are indeed the meanings of his own soul.

Then, if the consciousness can rise up to the next level called the Pleasing Self (*Nafs-i Mardhiyya*), he will have reached the point of actualizing the attributes of his essence (*dhat*)... This is the point of annihilation in Him, where the iceberg melts, and the one observing the meanings in himself becomes himself.

The truth is; the manifestation of these meanings on a person is a matter of **preordination** (*taqdir*).

What is of primary importance is an individual's **archetypal essence** (*a'yan thabita*); in other words, the meanings he has been created to actualize. The next stage is the **skills** and **capabilities** given unto him in order to fulfill this actualization. Then the encounter of the 'cause' will occur, that is, a subject who will render the means to actualize his archetype. When the individual submits his existence to this cause, and eventually annihilates himself in the cause and becomes **nothing**, his archetypal essence will manifest completely.

From the point to man...

From man to the point...

One who has diffused the boundaries of the **Pre-eternal** and **Post-eternal** One... One who, by actualizing the reality of his soul, has become nothing in the limitless and infinite nature of his soul!

When we refer to infinity, we are actually referring to the **World of Names**, for it is completely out of question to make any reference to the nature of His Absolute Essence (*dhat*).

He is infinite in terms of His meanings. Hence, even **His infiniteness** is an 'attribute'.

One cannot contemplate His Absolute Essence (*dhat*)!

In fact, even **His Oneness** (*Ahadiyyah*) is an attribute of **His Absolute Being.**

Notice that 'Allah' is the 'name' of a Being whose attributes we have been notified of.

Just as **'Hulusi'** is a name given to me, a name to reference my being, **'ALLAH'** is also a name we use to **reference His Absolute Essence. A name is merely a sign we use to indicate something.**

The extent to which the name **'Hulusi'** reveals the attributes and qualities I possess, whether I have manifested them or not, is the extent to which the name **'Allah'** can explain **His Magnificent Being.**

The Glorious Being who observes Himself on the mirror of the name 'Allah'!

Ideally, He observes Himself on the mirror of the name 'ALLAH' *through* **mankind.**

The Absolute Essence is beyond comprehension through definitions based on **attributes**. He, who attempts to bring a definition to the Absolute Essence, is an ignorant person, indirectly confessing his place amongst the 'imitators'. For he, who has been enlightened, will know without a doubt that in addressing the Absolute Essence, one can only go as far as His attributes.

No one has the liberty to talk about or define the **'nothingness'**, for nothingness is the place where all contemplations stop, where thoughts cease to be, where life, senses, words have no validity!

"Before He created the heavens and the earth, he was in *Ama*, the absolute potential. And He is as now as He ever was."

The place of nothingness is such an absolute darkness that everything one knows, thinks, and imagines becomes completely obsolete.

Let's hope **we are of those, or at least *amongst* those, who He has chosen for Himself.**

But beyond the conceptions of time and space, everything has already been lived and done! So what we need to do then is to pursue the path that best reflects our natural disposition and character, the path we find ourselves accessing with ease, rather than painstakingly going against our nature and making our lives difficult.

"Allah created Adam in His own image."

What does this mean?..

Man's existence is in accordance with divine existence. Man also has an essence. Man also has attributes, qualities and meanings that belong to his essence, and a place where he manifests his qualities, i.e., his body.

Just as we talk about an **Absolute Existence, Essence** (*dhat*), **Attribute, Names** (*asma*) **and Acts** (*af'al*), we can also talk about **the essence, attributes, names and acts of man**. Where, of course, the essence of man is ultimately derived from the Essence of the Absolute, as man does not possess a separate essence from the Absolute Essence of the One. Man's existence depends on the existence of the Absolute Essence.

The attributes of man can be summarized as follows; **life, knowledge, will, power, speech, hearing and sight.** In other words, man is *Hayy* (Living) *Aleem* (Knowing) *Mureed* (Willing) *Qadir* (Powerful) *Mutakallim* (Speaking) *Sami* (Perceiving) **and** *Basir* (Evaluating). This is because **man's existence depends on His existence, and therefore His attributes.**

Hence **Allah has created mankind in His own image, that is, in the image of His Names and Attributes.** There is no other existence in whose image He can create man. In any case, He encompasses the whole of existence; there is nothing other than He!

Every individual is a unique expression of a unique composition of His names. Due to this, there is multiplicity within unity. Though by essence we are all one and the same, our outward manifestations are varied. To put it allegorically, when the inward meanings of the One outwardly localizes and becomes dense at innumerable points, we have what appears to be the cosmos.

Each of these localized points, by essence and origin, are compositions of divine names, magnified and manifested on a grand scale. Thus, all of the galaxies and their constellations, with their stars and rays and so on, are just different compositions of the divine names. That is, they are all materializations of the compositional properties denoted by the divine names.

The Absolute Existence wanted to observe His meanings, and thus disclosed Himself through His Names, which eventually formed the 'world of forms'.

To illustrate this divine design, we can metaphorically think of it as localizations of the divine Names and meanings that transform into cosmic rays or angelic forces, which eventually form the world, as we know it.

Before any 'form' actually becomes physically manifest, its archetypal essence is defined, and based on this, its potential capabilities and skills are delegated.

In the sight of the Absolute Existence, forms are constant, as forms have essentially formed from compositions of His immutable Names and meanings.

However, at this point, we should take care to avoid a common misconception. That is, thinking of the Absolute Existence as a designer or a creator who is 'separate' from, or outside of, the world of forms.

Let's remember that a limitless boundless force encompasses the whole of existence. There is nothing other than this existence. Words like **'Him'** or **'His'** are only used here due to the limitation of language. Allah cannot be defined with words.

The relative existence, which we refer to as **'I'**, is ultimately our brain's projection of the compositions formed by His meanings.

This projection then utilizes the skills and capabilities, given to it, to fulfill its mission or reach the purpose for which it has been designed.

Our final destination is defined at the point of death where our brain stops functioning, and a transition takes place from this dimension and body to another.

How one lives defines how one will die. And how one lives is defined in their archetypal essence, which is reflected by the skills and capabilities we have been innately given (our natural disposition).

Our unique composition is made of the meanings of His Names.

The specific skills and capabilities, comprising our composition, guide us and engage us in certain actions and these actions then shape and design our spirit which becomes 'fixed' at the point of death, with which we continue our afterlife.

Hence, one's lifestyle, actions, personality and so on, will be shaped and defined by and according to the purpose for which he or she has been designed to accomplish, that is, the meaning he or she has been destined to manifest. [What begins as an archetypal essence flourishes and evolves, throughout one's lifetime, until finally getting fixed at the point of death.]

Every event, lived at every level of existence, is an expression of meanings that the One wishes to observe in Himself.

Every unit of existence will comply with the requirements of his make-up. By actualizing his unique composition, he will be effectuating his duty as a servant to Allah.

So, the meanings that form man are the meanings Allah wishes to observe in Himself.

All this said, **Allah is *Al-Ghani*** (The One who is beyond being labeled and limited by the manifestations of His Names, as He is Great [*Akbar*] and beyond all concepts) **and beyond any form or need.** Hence, **it is absolutely invalid to think of Allah as 'this meaning in that form', and restricting to say 'Allah is as such' or 'Allah is this much'.** Just as making a judgment about an artist, based on one out of perhaps thousands of his artworks, cannot be accepted!

If we can comprehend all that has been discussed here, then it would have become evident that we need to do all that it takes to accomplish our purpose in the best possible way.

If we consciously understand these truths then the probability is that we have also been equipped with the required skills to undergo the necessary transformations in the path to self-actualization.

It is said that:

"Allah will not permit his servant to make a prayer that He isn't willing to accept."

"If He has allowed His servant to make a particular prayer, then He will most assuredly answer his prayer."

If He has given us the capacity to comprehend these truths, then most probably it will be possible for us to live through the events that will actualize these meanings in us.

But first, we must purify our souls, cleanse ourselves from the conditionings of the 5 senses and make a leap to the higher dimensions of consciousness.

Praying, that is the process of directing our thought waves to this purpose, is our most powerful tool!

And if fulfilling our purpose has been **preordained**, then we're not going to have too much difficulty.

But what does **preordainment** or **divine discretion** actually mean?

6

THE DISCRETION OF THE ONE

The Topic of Fate (*qadar*) is the one topic that has captivated and occupied humanity throughout all time, and that only a select few, of a certain level of enlightenment, have been able to decipher...

In order to unravel **the mystery of fate**, one must first adopt and discern **the concept of Unity**.

So long as **the reality of Unity** isn't conscientiously understood and applied, one's acceptance of **fate** cannot surpass the level of blind faith.

This is precisely the reason why vicegerency has been given to humans, and not the jinn[12], who used to reign on earth before humans were created.

The jinn, though acquainted with almost all the mechanics of the system, are restricted from apprehending two core realities:

1. The mystery of Unity.

2. The mystery of fate.

---

[12] For more information on the "jinn" please refer to the book *Spirit Man Jinn* available on the website www.ahmedhulusi.org/en/

Because the jinn don't have the capacity to understand or carry these truths, humans were created with the necessary cognizance and capacity to fathom these mysteries.

Based on the verse;

"I'm going to create on earth (the body) **a caliph** (a vicegerent, who will live at the conscious awareness level of the Dimension of Names)**."** (Quran 2:30)

Humans were created with an innate capacity to comprehend the mysteries of **Unity** and **fate**, hence becoming worthy of **vicegerency.**

To apprehend Unity, one must first study the meaning of the **'Word of Unity'** (*Kalima-i Tawhid*), followed by an analysis and an evaluation of the meaning of the 112th chapter (*al-Ikhlas)* of the Quran.

It is impossible to understand the reality of **the Absolute Existence**, referred to with the name Allah, if we don't first absorb the meaning of chapter *al-Ikhlas*.

To **'READ'** the chapter *al-Ikhlas* does not mean to *merely repeat* the words in this short chapter. One may repeat the chapter *al-Ikhlas* 100,000 times without ever once 'READING' the verse **'Allah is One'. To read this verse means to understand, feel, and live its truth.**

As I said before, the word **'Allah'** is **a name**. There is a significant difference between calling upon one's name, and knowing the nature of the being called upon with that name, hence calling upon that **being** with that name! In one, you're merely uttering the words on the signpost, while in the latter; you're reading the signpost and actually travelling in the direction it gives.

Such 'travelers' are those who are **near to Allah** (*muqarribun*), referred to as the **People of Allah** (*ahlullah*). In other words, those who are mentioned in the verse,

"...Allah chooses for Himself whom He wills..." (Quran 42:13)

If we can comprehend the reality that the name ALLAH points to One body, not in the sense of a physical body, **but in the sense that there isn't a second being other than His Being, that His limitless, infinite Being encompasses all... And if we can understand that He hasn't come about from something, and due to His infinite nature, no 'other' thing has come about from Him... Then it may become obvious that an Infinite One, has contemplated, evaluated, manifested and then made nonexistent the whole of creation in His 'Knowledge'.**

To put it another way, with **His Knowledge** and Power, a Limitless, Infinite One has created the worlds from nothing, and observed the reflections of His Names via the names of the creation, **all at the level of knowledge!**

These 'forms of meanings' in the Knowledge of the One, obtain their form from His existence, by manifesting the properties of His Names, at His discretion. And it is He yet again, who observes these meanings.

A Being that encompasses all beings...

A cosmos that exists **at the level of knowledge...**

To give an example: Let us create a world in our imagination. Let us imagine all the different types of people living in this world... Despite how real it may feel to us, it is a world created from nothing in our imagination; it has no real substantial existence independent of our existence; it is eventually 'nonexistent'.

As such, all of the universes and all the dimensions and life forms that they contain exist in His Knowledge, depend on His existence, and are fundamentally nonexistent!

Comprehending this immense reality will enable us to see a remarkable truth. That is, **Allah** with the properties of the name **'The Possessor of Absolute Will'** (*Mureed*), has **willed** to create appropriate forms for the meanings to be manifested and observed. And these forms willingly conformed and accepted this duty.

Let us now go back to the Universe we created in our imagination. We imagined and populated a world with different individuals, equipping unique skills and capabilities to them. As such, these individuals, in our imagination, manifest their essence **based on the skills they have been given**. Can we say then, that these individuals have their *own independent will*, with which they choose to govern their actions?

Or is it more correct to say, these imaginary individuals are projecting the innate characteristics that we have assigned to them? Let us suppose that one of these individuals commit murder and kill another individual, whereby a third person who witnesses this scene says "So and so has killed so and so". But all of this is happening at the level of our knowledge, in our thoughts and imagination. We are writing the script and ordaining their roles, and they are playing it out. So how can we say **"So and so has killed so and so *with his own independent free will and choice*"? Saying this would entail the assumption that 'all' individuals have a free will, and render obsolete the Will of the One.** The declaration of a free will alongside the Will of the One will implicitly fragment and lessen His Absolute Will.

In his book, ***Huccetullahi'l Baligha***, Sheikh Veliullah Dihlevi, who is generally known to be the reviver (*mujaddid*) of the generation after Imam Rabbani, says:

> *"People can choose their actions, but this apparent choice is never real as it is divinely motivated by certain benefits and payoffs making the person think it's their choice, whereas in reality it's the Divine discretion in disguise."*

HENCE, "...THEY HAVE NO CHOICE..." (Quran 28:68)

Muhammad (saw) says:

"The hearts are in between Allah's two fingers, He shapes the hearts as He wishes."

Ibrahim Hakki Erzurumi, known to be **the Great Helper** (*ghaus*) of his time, says in his ***Marifetname***:

> *"The pre-eternal discretion is above and greater than the causes, as an individual cannot request something after Allah provides it.*

As such, Allah's provision is the cause for everything, and nothing is the cause or the reason for His provision. His blessings are not from you. Where were you when His blessings came to you?

All things rely on His wish, while His wish relies on nothing. For, Allah does as He wishes. The verse 'Allah does as He wills'[13] informs us that everything comes about from His will and power."

There are numerous Quranic verses and sayings of **Muhammad (saw)** to elucidate this topic. I don't want to repeat all of them here[14], but here are 2 verses to reinforce the matter:

"No calamity befalls you on earth (on your body and outer world) **or among yourselves** (your inner world) **that has not already been recorded in a book** (formed in the dimension of knowledge) **before We bring it into being! Indeed for Allah, this is easy."**

"We inform you of this in order that you don't despair over your losses or exult (in pride) **over what We have given you, for Allah does not like the boastful and the arrogant!"** (Quran 57:22-23)

To understand the core of the matter, we must view the 'outer' situation from the 'inner' point of essence; we must view multiplicity from the point of unity. If we try and view in reverse, that is, if we try and view the peak point of the pyramid from its bottom layer, our vision is bound to get obscured somewhere along the way, and we are bound to get sidetracked by all the details and miss the Essence.

The sole condition one must fulfill, in order to grasp and solve this mystery from its core, is to view the 'many' from the point of the 'One', to view the manifestations from the point of the Essence, not the other way around. In doing so, one will inevitably see that

---

[13] Quran 2:253
[14] Please refer to the books *The Mysteries of Man* and *Mind and Faith* for more information.

the 'outer' existence, that is the conceptual world of forms, is nothing but a projection of the implicit meanings in His Knowledge!

All life forms acquire their life from His Life.

He is *Aleem*. Hence all knowledge pertaining to creation is from, and within, His Knowledge. Allah's Knowledge is limitless and infinite.

He is *Mureed*. His Will is infinite. Hence, all outward expressions of will are from His Will, becoming manifest in accordance to the compositions of Names they carry in their essence.

When we view an activity of an individual we say *"he is acting out of his free will"*. **Whereas this outward display of will is in reality nothing more than the disclosure of the Will of the One through that individual; just as the water that runs from a particular tap isn't different than the water in the reservoir.**

The application of the same principle to all His other names and attributes, such as **Power, Speech, Hearing, Sight** and so on, renders evident the truth that Allah encompasses 'all'.

We can conclude then, that there is only one life in the whole of existence, and that is the life of **the** Ever-Living One (*Hayy*). And again, there is only one will in the whole of the cosmos, and that is *Mureed* (the Possessor of Absolute Will). If the Will of the One is infinite and limitless, then how can we fragment His eternal will by assigning a partial, individualized will to creation?

He is the All-Powerful One, thus, all expressions of power pertain to His Power. Every appearance of meaning, and all the acts of every atom in existence, can all be traced to the boundless, all-encompassing names that manifest the Knowledge of the One.

Hence, there is only one **Will**, one **Power**, and one **infinite Knowledge** to direct this Will and Power pertinent to **the One represented by the name Allah.**

He reveals and observes Himself on the mirror of the name Allah, yet at the same time He declares:

"Verily, Allah (in terms of His Absolute Essence) **is *Ghani* from** (being conditioned and limited by) **the worlds**

(individualized and materialized compositions of His Names)." (Quran 29:06)

ALLAH is Pre-eternal and Post-eternal (*Baqi*).

All the worlds are like seemingly transitory waves coming from nothingness and going to nothingness in the ocean of Eternity.

We too are like a wave, forming in and from the ocean and returning to it. As **all things will return to their source**, so too every formed wave will return to its formless state in the ocean and **not be!**

In the sight of the knowledgeable ones, even waves don't exist.

A day will come and we will finally realize that we are **'not'**. Our assumed selves will be annihilated in the existence of Allah, and then the fire of our internal hell will be extinguished. Who will we see in the mirror then, I wonder?

Will the mirror be the Eternal One and 'the self' be naught?

In reality, it is absurd to talk about the nothingness of naught. It is as its name suggests naught! Hence for the enlightened one, there is in every instant nothing but the Eternal One. In fact, for the enlightened one, there is no 'every instant' and there is only 'one instant'.

Eventually, these things can only be lived and experienced, but to sum up what has been discussed:

In order to evaluate existence in a proper context, we must view existence as though looking from the tip of a cone. That is, from the point of unity going toward multiplicity, from the inner core to the outer shell, not the other way around.

Since the illimitable, infinite Being has no limit, there can be no other existence than His but His infiniteness needs to be recognized in terms of his infinite attributes.

We have always attempted to explain His infinite nature in terms of His Absoluteness, now we need to recognize His infinite nature in respect of His attributes. In doing so, we will recognize **His infinite Life, Knowledge, Will, Power** and we will understand that the so-called '*free-will*' that we associate to ourselves is only a product of our 5 senses. Once we grasp the fundamental reality that our apparent free-will isn't 'free' from His Will, we can stop dividing the Whole into fragments and become cognizant of the verse:

> **"Do not turn toward gods** (exterior manifestations of power) **other than Allah."** (Quran 28:88)

If we have been ordained to comprehend His Infiniteness, not just in terms of His Absolute Being but also in terms of his attributes and His whole Existence, then we will realize that **fate** is nothing but the **field of observing manifest upon the wish of the One.**

7

THE OBSERVING ONE

The Observing One!

Since He is the Observer, then the meanings and forms, that He wishes to observe, must be the product of His wish...

Viewing things from this perspective, the whole of existence appears to be the **life, knowledge, will, power, speech, hearing and sight of the One...**

While everything in creation is incapacitated with impotence in the sight of the One with Absolute Power, the only thing this Exalted Being doesn't have is 'impotence'.

The Perfect Man (*Al-Insan Al-Kamil*) is referred to with an expression of impotence in the verse:

> **"...Indeed, he is cruel** (insufficient in duly living his reality) **and ignorant** (of the knowledge of His infinite Names)." (Quran 33:72)

The whole of creation is like an extension of the **Perfect Man.** Nevertheless, he is limited with finiteness in the sight of the Infinite One. Hence, he is impotent.

The Creator that is the One who has manifested countless forms in creation, has indeed created the worlds in impotence. The Perfect Man is unrestricted in terms of his infinite potential and in respect to the **Absolute Unknown** (*gayb-i mutlaq*). However, he is impotent and restricted in terms of the implicitness of the meanings he manifests. **Ibn al-Arabi** references this impotence with his words:

> *"I have found the rank of the 'Impotent Servant' to be the highest of ranks."*

This state of the **'impotent servant'** is essentially the *state of observing for* the Perfect Man.

We should take care not to interpret these notions with our human minds lest we fall into human errors and misconceive the reality.

Know that, in the sight of **the Perfect Man**, compared to that which hasn't yet manifested, all manifestations are limited, and limitation is an implication of impotence.

In this light, **Muhammad's (saw)** words **"I repent 70 times a day"** bears the awareness of this limitation. That is, the repentance of the Perfect Man is in reference to the impotence he feels in regards to illimitably manifesting the unlimited, unrestricted meanings of the One.

In other words, it is his way of declaring: **"As the requirement of my servitude to you, I am impotent of reflecting your illimitable meanings"** thereby confessing His Omnipotence over the corporeal worlds.

Such are the contemplations of the Perfect Man...

But if Allah wills, He can also speak through a servant like me to impart these teachings. Whether he chooses a sultan or a servant, it is His wish and command, and there is no limit or restriction to the favors of the Exalted One. Our duty is to take the teaching, appraise and understand it, if this has been meant for us, of course.

Otherwise, based on the verse,

> **"Each will act in accordance to his creation program** (*fitrah*-natural disposition)." (Quran 17:84)

If we are not meant to comprehend these teachings, we will effectuate the dictum **'Each will do what has been made easy** (by nature) **for him'** and chase after the destiny we find easy, deprived of these realities.

8

DOES CREATION DETERMINE KNOWLEDGE?

For centuries, scholars have argued over the question:

"Is creation determined by precedent knowledge, or is knowledge determined by the creation?"

Or in other words, does something become known after it outwardly manifests and discloses itself, or does it become manifest based on the knowledge that exists before it's disclosed?

The answer to this question elucidates the mystery of creation...

Let's suppose creation exists 'independently'. The 'knowledge', pertaining to creation, is nevertheless part of Allah's Knowledge. Now, if it is a **must** for Allah to outwardly manifest His Knowledge, then one can say **'knowledge is determined by manifestation'**.

But since we're talking about an unlimited, infinite Being manifest in every dimension, an illimitable Absolute Existence, who is not only infinite in terms of His Absoluteness but also in regards to His attributes, then we're looking at an infinite display of Names and their explicit Acts!

What can exist outside of, and hence become a subject of, dependency for the One who is infinite by way of His Absoluteness, Attributes, Names and Acts? How can He be dependent on, or be determined by, a manifestation that originates from His Knowledge in the first place?

We say **'absolute power belongs to Allah alone'** but seldom do we contemplate its true meaning.

Let us try and employ an abstract view on things by cleansing ourselves from our conditionings, so that we may perhaps 'melt our iceberg' in the objectiveness of consciousness and attain selflessness. Let us become 'naught' in the ocean of reality, and realize that the whole of manifestation, everything that has come into creation or that will come into creation, depends on, and is determined by knowledge!

Some claim;

"He manifests what He finds in His Knowledge; that is, the meanings that are implicit in His existence become explicit through manifestation, hence, meanings cause their own creation..."

However, the key point, missing in this view, is that Allah manifests the meanings He 'wishes' to observe, not what He feels 'obliged' to. Allah doesn't outwardly express the meanings that he finds in His Knowledge, **but the meanings He creates with the knowledge pertaining to His Absolute Essence.**

Claiming otherwise imposes delimitation to **Allah's Infinite Self** and implies the condition that Allah must be the sum total of all explicit meanings, whereas Allah is **One** (*Ahad*). Just as **'Allah isn't made of parts or compositions of parts'**, Allah isn't an accumulation of meanings either. We can't define Him as a formation of Names. It is the meanings formed by the **'attribute of knowledge'** pertaining to Allah's Absolute Essence (*dhat*) that we're referring to here. Hence, **Allah manifests what He 'wishes'.** This does not, in any way, connote a physical or a spiritual 'form' to Allah, as He is far beyond need of forms.

If Allah needs to manifest something in His Knowledge, then this must have an implicit form at the level of Knowledge, before coming into physical manifestation. However, Allah has created the worlds based on the meanings He created in His Knowledge, as Allah is free to govern His Knowledge as He wishes to.

The worlds, which are inexistent in respect of their reality, have not been created in respect of the Acts of Allah but in respect of the Names of Allah. Hence, the whole of existence is present in His Knowledge.

Those, who fall into the misunderstanding that 'knowledge is determined by manifestation', try to view the top from the bottom. That is, they try to solve the mystery with the knowledge and light of **Minor Sainthood** (*Wilayat Sughra*). **Minor Sainthood** involves **'ascension'** from the people to Allah, whereas Major Sainthood (*Wilayat Kubra*) involves the condescension of Allah to the level of the people.

In the sight of the Perfect Man, who maintains the knowledge and the excellence of divine disclosure at the station of eternity (*BakaBillah*), **manifestation is determined by knowledge!**

Contrary to this, **based on the view of ascension in the sight of Minor Sainthood, knowledge is determined by manifestation**, as in this view manifestation appears to be **fixed.**

When viewed from the level of Major Sainthood, the quintessence of disclosing **the Knowledge of Allah** (*Nubuwwat*), nothing exists anyway, other than **the Absolute Essence** (*dhat*). Hence, it is said that the Absolute Essence manifests, from nothing, the meanings He wishes to observe in the Knowledge from Himself, to Himself. Of course, here we are referring to the meanings of the Names of Allah, not the Acts of Allah.

Allah creates the meanings, and then discloses them through manifestation. At every instant, these manifested meanings interact with each other in accordance to their properties, and based on this, they perceive one another as the Acts of Allah. Although I said **'every instant'**, let's remember that in reality there is only **'one'** instant, as the whole of manifestation is the result of **a single theophany**, what the Sufi's call **One Theophany** (*Tajalli Wahid*) or **a Single Disclosure. All has begun and ended at the 'point';** *alif* **and the rest are just an illusion.**

Pertaining to the level of knowledge, there are meanings of Names, which have come into existence though the act of creation, referred to by the verse:

"**Verily, Allah** (in terms of His Absolute Essence) **is *Ghani* from** (being conditioned and limited by) **the worlds** (individualized and materialized compositions of His Names)." (Quran 29:06)

The fact, that knowledge isn't determined by manifestation, is evident in **Allah's Self-Sufficiency** (*Ghani*) and **Independence of the worlds** and **the meanings of the Names** from which they derive. If knowledge was determined by creation, then the verse **"Allah is free from need of the worlds"** would be rendered obsolete, as this would suggest a form of dependency on the worlds.

Whereas, Allah, **being free from need and independent of the worlds**, is indicative of the Absoluteness of Allah's Essence (*dhat*) referred by the Sufis as **the pure and absolute essence** (*dhat-i baht*).

The truth is, **Allah's Absolute Essence** (*dhat*) cannot even be defined as **'Absoluteness'** as this word is used merely as an indicator to the Absolute Essence (*dhat*) in relevance to lower levels of manifestation. In reality, the **'Essence'** cannot be expounded with terms such as **'absoluteness', 'purity'** or **'existence'.**

If we can truly fathom this fundamental reality, then we will be able to view the topic from the top of the cone, from the point of unity.

Isn't the event, known as 'the Big Bang', a simulation of the same concept on a macro level? The event, called the Big Bang, is a result of **white matter** that forms from **white holes**... All of the universes in the cosmos were born from such singular 'points' and have expanded into what they appear to be today. That first point is the defining point of the end. Just as the first cell of an elephant, for example, also contains the information of its last cell.

Hence, just as the innumerable expressions of existence in the cosmos have all originated from one primary point, all of the 'meanings' in all the worlds have originated from **the Knowledge of Allah**, based on **His Infinite and Illimitable Will and Power.**

If we can approach the matter in this way, we will have a clearer understanding of **'fate'.**

Allah says **"I created humans as vicegerents on earth"** and **"Man is the vicegerent on earth"**.

There are **vicegerents in the heavens**, that is, **all other dimensions** in the universe too. Every dimension, according to its structure and capacity, contains its own vicegerents. What we know of a vicegerent is the one delegated to earth, limited by earthly restrictions. There is only **'one' real vicegerent** however, and that is what the Sufis call **the Perfect Man** (*Al-Insan Al-Kamil*) in reference to **the Grand Spirit** (*Ruh-ul Azam*). Also known as **The Reality of Muhammad** (*Hakikat-i Muhammadiyyah*) and in respect of knowledge as **The First Intellect** (*Aql-i Awwal*).

Adam is the miniature of this Grand Spirit. Interestingly, the word Adam literally means **'naught'**. He has a name but his existence is **naught!** Like the Roc bird, its name exists but its self doesn't!

We've already established that the perceivable existence, in respect of its essence, is Allah's anyway... It has expanded and **multiplied via His Names, as the Names, or their expressions and manifestations increased, existence appeared also to multiply!** Whereas **in terms of 'Unity'** (*wahidiyyah*)**, existence is only 'One'**.

If we were to give each wave a separate name, it wouldn't change the fact that they are all waves. Whether some are bigger or smaller, whether some appear to be more curved or not, they are all waves in the same ocean. This is precisely where variations of perception originate. Perceptions differ according to views (*basirah*). If you view things from above, there appears to be neither any differences nor any dispute, neither alteration nor altercation.

"Knowledge was one point. The ignorant ones multiplied it" says Hadhrat Ali...

As such, while relaying his words, I'm altogether displaying my own ignorance by the lengthiness of my discussion. Albeit, displaying my ignorance reveals at the same time the perfection of the 'Perfected Ones', as all things are known through their opposites. If a thing doesn't have an opposite, its worth and value cannot be known. All things have been created in pairs, one opposing the other, one *relevant* to the other.

The amalgamation of opposites can only occur at the point of 'Unity'.

And Unity can only be viewed by removing the curtains that veil it; the curtains that are from itself to itself.

The Absolute Essence whose name *Wahid* (The One) denotes His attribute *Wahidiyyah* (Unity), has manifested with the qualities of the Dimension of Attributes, by respect of His *Rahmaniyyah* (the infinite potential from which divine Names emanate). With these qualities then, He has established the sovereignty of the Names at the Dimenson of *Malikiyyah* (Divine Dominion). In turn, these names have become outwardly explicit in the World of Acts (*af'al*) in accordance to the creeds of His *Rububiyyah*, in the form of unique composition of Names.

Every entity, or instance of manifestation, carries, in itself, all of the compositional qualities of this chain of evolution.

Muhammad (saw) says: **"The particle is the same as the whole"**; pointing to the reality of **the holographic universe.**

The particle derives its essence, attributes and qualities from the Essence, Attributes and Qualities of the Infinite One. The acts of the particle are the conversion of these implicit divine qualities into explicit manifestations.

Viewing things from this angle, one cannot see anything other than the One.

We say the dimension of Allah's Acts, the dimension of Names, the dimension of His Absolute Essence and so on... But what exactly do we understand by the word **'dimension'? Where is the dimension of Names in respect to the Acts? Where are the Attributes in respect to the Names?**

They place the 'Chair' (*Kursi*) **on the 7 heavens, and the 'Throne'** (*arsh*) **upon the *Kursi*, then search for a god within these defined parameters, whereas "He is present with His Essence in every particle".**

Allah's Absolute Essence (*dhat*) is Infinite, so if **He is present with His Infinite Self in every particle, within every dimension,** then there is no particle in reality, **there is only the Eternal One.**

As long as we fall short of fully comprehending Allah's Limitlessness in respect of His 'One'-ness (*Wahidiyyah*), our understanding of **Islam and faith** will always be less than adequate.

The Quran depicts the state of such people as:

> **"Did you not see the one who has deified his '*hawa*'** (instinctual desires, bodily form, illusionary self)**?"** (Quran 25:43)

People have created a god in their imagination based on their own conditionings, and they are squandering their lives worshipping this imaginary god!

To be free from becoming one of these people **we must comprehend, observe, feel and live the Limitlessness of Allah in respect of His Oneness** (*Wahidiyyah*).

All of these can only be understood via experience, not through reading, but through living.

To live it duly, one must be initiated by a cause. One must be able surpass the words and become the actualization of their meanings. One must then escape the veils of existence, until there remains only the Observer.

To achieve this, one must first **believe** and then to pursue his belief. One must be cleansed and purified from all his conditionings and the emotions that are attached to them.

Once this happens, one will inevitably fall into consumption of **his natural instincts and bodily desires.** Thus, one must take extra caution to keep his bodily temptations under strict supervision.

After this is achieved, one must then demolish the illusion of **a separate 'Self'** and **"Die before dying"** as the Sufis say, that is become naught and realize **the Eternal One is Allah.**

After all of this, **one may finally escape thinking as a man and begin thinking as Allah**, as Jesus says.

9

THE ANTICHRIST

Many of us come to a point where we think we've escaped our conditionings. Little do we realize that even while we say "I am no longer conditioned", we are still saying "I am"!

Engulfed by the illusion of a 'self', we become captives of our bodies, and hence subjugated to the **'antichrist of the illusory-self'**. Subservient to every bodily temptation and desire, we begin paving our paths to destruction.

After eliminating the conditionings during the stage of maturation and development, one becomes subject to a certain amount of freedom. Now, if one hasn't also eliminated the illusion of the 'self' during this process, then the newly gained freedom works to serve the body. One becomes consumed by all sorts of bodily appetites, leading ultimately to the deification of their body.

Consequently, one begins living in the **'paradise of the antichrist'**. That is, as opposed to the 'Absolute' self, the 'illusory' self becomes the dominating force, and by obeying the illusory self, one inevitably gets choked in the swamp of their illusion.

Let's reflect for a moment…

If **the Reviver** (*Mujaddid*), of the period between the *Hijri* years 1400-1410, was the last reviver, then following **the *Mahdi***

(Saviour), **the Antichrist** should appear and claim to be God round about these times, after which **Jesus** should come back to the world!

Of course, this is the explicit manifestation of the matter. Those, who can't grasp this reality, either deny it altogether or start making all sorts of interpretations... Whether one can fathom this reality or not, it will come to be.

However, there is also an implicit side, to which I would like to draw your attention.

When the **Mahdi** within is awakened, we will have attained selflessness and realized our apparent existence is really His existence... This knowledge-based realization will be inadequate though, for without a thorough purification, we will still be subject to our **inner antichrist**'s infamous command: **"I am your Lord, serve me!"** Naturally, we will begin to think this is the voice of Allah, and start believing our 'self' is Allah, while still identifying 'ourselves' as our body.

As a result of this false identification, our dominant thought will become: **"Since I am God (or the manifestation of God), I am free to do whatever I like in this body!"** thus accrediting all forms of bodily pleasures to ourselves.

This is why **Muhammad (saw)** says:

> **"When the antichrist emerges, the believers should run from his paradise into his hell..."**

> **"Expressing the inverted reality that the antichrist's seemingly pleasurable paradise is in actuality hell itself!"**

Bodily desires are generally expressed as 'natural' desires. Some even attribute these to the **'soul'** (*nafs*) and claim such behavior pertains to the soul, whereas what we mean by the soul is simply the ego; the sense of **'I'**. **When the soul is veiled from this reality, it falsely identifies itself with the physical body, hence attributing all bodily states, desires, etc. to itself.**

To clarify the matter a little further, let's temporarily use the word **'consciousness'**, in place of the word **'soul'**. When our consciousness is at this lower state of frequency, we become occupied primarily with the pursuit of bodily pleasures, thus preventing the soul from actualizing its reality.

Many people have faltered at this point and indeed have fallen into the pharaoh-like state of the ego, attributing divinity to themselves and succumbing to physical pleasures or addictions, eventually causing their own demise.

The first strike to the antichrist comes from the *Mahdi*.

Mahdi is **the guide** to the truth. That is to say, it is **knowledge** that counteracts the antichrist. The knowledge of the truth stands up against the illusory self and says:

"Do not be confused by the belief you have derived from your illusion, that your soul is God with your physical body. Your consciousness is an abstract concept! Your body, on the other hand, is a physical being bound to the conditions of the physical dimension in which it resides. Abandon the false belief that you are your body and realize that you are far beyond the body; you are consciousness!"

This calling does not always eradicate the antichrist's claim: **"I am God; I'm free to live as I please"**. Thus, it becomes necessary for Jesus to descend from the heavens, or in other words, to emerge from the implicit realm to the explicit realm, in order to kill the antichrist! Despite the fact that the Mahdi emerges with the Knowledge of Reality, it isn't sufficient to exterminate the antichrist of the illusory-self, not until Jesus descends from the heavens and disposes with divine Power!

Jesus, descending from the heavens, is symbolic of divine power opposing the antichrist, i.e. the illusory-self, or, the fake identity. As **Muhammad (saw)** says:

"Upon encountering Jesus, the Antichrist will become extinguished immediately."

That is to say, when divine power becomes disclosed, the act of **'dying before death'** becomes manifest and the realization becomes ever clear, that we are only existent in terms of our consciousness.

Thereafter, we become enabled to forego our attachment to our bodies, ascending our consciousness to the saintly state at the level of The Contented Self (*Nafs-i Mutmainna*).

This is the point when the illusory self no longer defines itself as a body, and what the Sufis refer to as 'uniting with Allah' occurs.

Instead of interpreting the 'antichrist' as a figure expected to emerge before the major doomsday of the world, we may interpret it as a state of the illusory self that can befall us before our own doomsday, that is, our own death. Then, within this context, we can decipher what it means for the *Mahdi* (Saviour) to oppose, and for Jesus to defeat, the antichrist with divine power. Of course all of these are symbolic concepts. *Mahdi* represents the Islamic knowledge of Unity (*tawhid*) which is the equilibrium of Allah's incomparability (*tanzih*) and similarity (*tashbih*).

The Antichrist (*dajjal*) represents the excess of *tashbih* and an incorrect evaluation of it, leading one's consciousness to the belief "I am God" and the attempt to experience this within the plane of the body.

Jesus, on the other hand, being the one who has revealed the reality of *tashbih* to humanity in person, assumes the role of the 'corrector' of possible deviations. In Sufism, Jesus symbolizes the state of 'closeness' (*yaqeen*) to Allah, also known as the disclosure of Allah's power.

Upon appropriately comprehending these truths, we can attain the realization of our 'nothingness', as disclosed by the knowledge of Unity (*wahdat*), and kneel with our heads in prostration and pray:

"Oh Allah, please endow us with an enlightened lifestyle... elucidate, facilitate and simplify this for us!"

As **Muhammad (saw)** says:

"The most pleasing and acceptable prayer is the one made in prostration" and **"the closest place one may get to Allah is at the point of prostration."**

Since this is the case, then let us all place our heads on the floor in prostration. Will we have really prostrated by doing this? Yes, but only in form! Real prostration isn't a formal *imitation,* but the conscious awareness of one's 'nothingness' and the acknowledgement of Allah's 'Infiniteness'.

One, who prostrates with this awareness, observes the Infinite One through his poverty and **selflessness.** However, the former prostrates in shape, but erects his ego ever so uprightly, reminiscent of the state of those mentioned as "their backs will be like wood, they will not be able to prostrate, and every time they try they will roll over and fall"!

Indeed, **'prostration'** is the state of **'nothingness'**, which can only be attained by eliminating one's false and illusory identity. Such a person's prostration is like a unity with Allah, a divine closeness. In this state, a person will be like an observer, as divine attributes reveal themselves and divine power manifests, he will observe them in prostration.

It may also be appropriate to mention the act of **'bowing'** (*ruqu*) here.

As known, previous to Islam, methods of worship included both the standing position (*qiyam*) and prostration. *Ruqu* however, or the bowing position was introduced by **Muhammad (saw)** as part of *salah* (5 daily prayers).

Why though? What does bowing represent; why is it important?

Bowing in *salah* is the act of bending the body forward from the waist by an approximate 90 degrees, such that one is standing straight waist-down, but kneeling forward waist-up, like forming a right angle. But what does this mean?

Reciting the *Basmalah* and the *Fatiha* (the opening chapter of the Quran), in the upright position, is the act of attesting to the truth that 'uprightness' is only possible and appropriate when applied as the vicegerent of Allah. To not read these verses is a form of associating partnership with Allah (shirk), where one runs the risk of indirectly associating his own being as a partner to Allah.

Contrarily, prostration is the renunciation of the self and the declaration of **"I am not, You are!"**

'Bowing' then is the middle point of both positions and it is the declaration "I know that I am naught, I know intellectually that I'm inexistent and that only You exist, but this knowledge isn't sufficient to eliminate my identity and enable me to have a practical experience of this reality, due to this, I ask for your forgiveness…"

The knowledge of Unity (*wahdat*) was not imparted to previous communities; this higher reality was exposed to Muhammad's community (to the people of today). This being said, it was also conspicuous that not everyone will achieve the exuberant experience of true prostration. Hence, out of compassion, bowing was given as an alternative so that those who may not be able to experience the reality of prostration can at least bow down in humility, and intellectually accept their nothingness.

At the state of *closeness* to Allah, when the disclosure of divine attributes takes place during prostration, any wish is Allah's command. As;

"Indeed, Our word to a thing when We intend it to be, is to say 'Be,' and it is." (Quran 16:40)

Since this is the case, let us turn to **Allah.**

Let us pray to be protected from the Antichrist of the illusory self and the captivity of our fake identity. Let's ask to be bestowed with the enlightenment of His Reality and Unity. And whatever state or addiction may be impeding our spiritual growth let's genuinely 'want' to be freed from its enslavement, so that we may finally rise in consciousness and Unite with the One.

10

THE WILL OF THE ONE

When the One, **in order to experience Himself**, wills to divulge Self-disclosure through a particular form in the corporeal world, that form, will turn to the One at the expense of everything, including its own being. The sole purpose, of this particular form, will be to reach the One.

In order to achieve this goal, he will give up everything, from the plane of thoughts to the plane of actions, everything he assumes he owns will become expendable. He will forego his conditionings, and all the so-called values attached to them, and their resulting emotions... He will even aim to detach from his physical desires and addictions, cleansing his body from smoking or drinking habits, excessive eating or sleeping and any other bodily weaknesses he may have acquired in his lifetime. He will then commence spiritual practices to raise his consciousness.

As he discovers his reality at the level of consciousness, he will become cognizant of the One and realize all knowledge pertains to Him. He will then recognize the illusory nature of his self and the inexistence of his ostensible identity, and begin to let it go, finally annihilating himself and uniting with the One.

Nonetheless, all of this can only be achieved through the guidance of an enlightened mentor, already **living** this reality. For it is not possible for one to break free, from the confinements of certain conditionings, desires and natural tendencies, or the illusion of a self-identity, all by himself.[15]

So if he is to reach the One, he will seek out and find a guide who will enable him to relinquish all his conditionings, a guide who has already been through this process and has been enlightened. As one can't teach another how to swim, if they don't know how to swim themselves! If a man, who has never once seen the ocean, claims he can *teach you how to swim*, leave him in his delusion and continue your journey. A shepherd can't teach you how to swim. One must seek the right guidance from the right source.

Once the right guide is found and his guidance is heard and applied, purification of the soul will take place and the consciousness will be awakened. This arduous process will continue to until complete submission and unity with the One is attained. At this point, one will realize he is 'Islam'. He will become *'Abdullah'* that is **'the servant of Allah'** and reflect the meanings of Allah on his newly polished and purified mirror of selflessness.

True purification costs everything. It requires the sacrifice of everything we own. If we are not willing to give up all that we possess in this pursuit, it is probably best that we don't embark on this journey at all, for it is a journey filled with struggle, pain, tribulations and sufferings... It may cost our belongings, our loved ones, our identity and everything that is attached to it!

If we claim to be up to the challenge now, but cry in agony or play the blame game as soon as we encounter an apparent loss, not only will we not gain anything we seemingly lost, but also we will have become increasingly susceptible to enacting the very thing with which we blamed others.

Muhammad (saw) says:

"Do not criticize; you will not die until you experience what you have criticized."

---

15 This topic has been covered in detail in my book *Know Yourself.*

So, if we accept this knowledge and want to attain it, then we must be willing to burn in hell in order to get to heaven. For one can only be purified by burning! Just as gold is purified by fire…

> **"Indeed, Allah has purchased, from the believers, their souls (*nafs*) and their properties** [in exchange] **for that they will have Paradise."** (Quran 9:111) says the verse…

Note that it says **'souls'** and **'properties'**!

Let's evaluate these words in a broad term.

How can we both pursue bodily pleasures, allowing **the antichrist of the ego** to run his sovereignty at full capacity, and unite with the One? Clearly this is not possible. The Satan (ego) channels our thoughts to all sorts of 'cul-de-sac' avenues, making us think there is a way through, but alas, it is a trap of the ego; it is merely an assumption!

History is full of spiritually enlightened figures. Look at their lives. Which one has lived a life without any suffering? Their lives were full of purification and sacrifice!

We can only get as far as we forego from our identities. The amount of sacrifice, made from our 'selves', is the degree to which we can attain true reality. So, before the system inevitably and forcibly confiscates our possessions, belongings, loves ones, etc., why not willingly abandon them, first by detaching them from our egos and identities, and by purifying our hearts from material possessions and attachments?

In reality, everyone goes through similar experiences in life; everyone suffers the grief of loss, for example. However, the difference between just anyone, and one who has consciously willed to be awakened, is that the latter knows the wisdom behind it, and hence employs serenity and submission. The latter knows why he is burning and suffering, and chooses to do so with tranquility, while the former intensifies his pain with constant criticism and complaint.

But this isn't the prerequisite to enter heaven!

To unite with Allah, one must awaken his consciousness!

One may claim: "Just going to heaven is good enough for me" but this has already been determined on the 120th day after conception when we were decreed to be either of the **fortunate** (*said*) or the **unfortunate** (*shaqi*) ones.

If we were decreed to be **fortunate**, then all of its necessities will have been sent to us during our lifetime. We would have been endowed with the understanding and the knowledge, the thirst for the quest, the faith and its outward manifestation, finally resulting at the gates of heaven.

If, on the other hand, we have been decreed to be of the **unfortunate** ones, then:

"Allah is the owner of everything; He is All-Just and is free to do as He wishes. None has the right to question His wish!"

Who and what is independent of, or separate from, Allah such that they can question His authority?

If you claim you want the Reality, then you must be willing to pay the price my friend!

What if you are making this claim, yet deceiving yourself by continuing to indulge in personal pleasures?

Do not be veiled!

When Moses went to meet His *Rabb*, Allah called out to him from fire:

"I am Allah your *Rabb* O Moses!"

So do not be surprised when fire addresses you! Fire will burn you!

Do not be veiled from it when it addresses you from a place that burns you! What burns you is 'fire', not what your eyes perceive as 'flame'. And as long as you burn, you will be in your personal hell. This world is a part of hell too. So long as you continue living this **worldly** life, you will be living in hell.

Nevertheless, if you still claim you want to reach Allah, know that 'you' can never reach Allah.

Don't follow the footsteps of those who promise to give you a wonderful worldly life. Follow those who will **"Kill you before your death"**; lest you get addressed with the words **"You are forbidden to see me!"**

Those who provide you with a glittery worldly life will do so up to the grave, if that! Eventually, your demise will be inevitable.

Your true friend is the one who will kill you before you die, as 'the believer unites with Allah through death' at which point you will claim like Rumi:

> *"Do not despair at my funeral! Play and rejoice! For I am going to unite with my Beloved!"*

Indeed, your true friend is the one who will kill your fake identity, your illusory self, and save you from your illusion of being separate, hence enabling you to unite with your source.

Seek this death, and seek this friend, so that you can start truly living!

Death, like hell, is a mercy. The mercy of *Rahman* is hidden in suffering, just like remedy is hidden in bitter medicine.

Death only scares those who are attached to the world, as death for them means the loss of everything they seemingly own. But if one fails to deal with these fears now, the consequences, that it will bring tomorrow, will be much more formidable.

Come my friend... come willingly and lovingly to die for the sake of Allah so that you will be enlivened with **The Ever Living One** (*Hayy*) and **The Everlasting One** (*Baqi*).

Die now my friend, die now and live forever...

11

SO WHAT EXACTLY IS GOING ON IN OUR BRAIN?

In his *The Holographic Universe*, Michael **Talbot** presents the theories of Bohm and Pribram, and in reference to their proposed new way of looking at the world, he says:

> *"Our brains mathematically construct objective reality by interpreting frequencies that are ultimately projections from another dimension, a deeper order of existence that is beyond both space and time: The brain is a hologram enfolded in a holographic universe."*[16]

Let's try and understand the implications of this powerful view.

First of all, let's put time and space aside, and focus on the words:

> *"...a deeper order of existence from another dimension."*

A **'deeper'** order is the order within the depths of our existence; our essence, in Sufi terms, the **Absolute Existence!**

Beyond the illusory existence that we refer to when we say **'I'**, exists another **'I'**, one that is common to all existence, the Absolute **'I', the Absolute Self!**

---

[16] Talbot, 1991

The brain, then, is the converter of the frequencies that are projections from this Absolute 'I', who projects the frequencies of His implicit meanings that He wants to disclose!

I cannot adequately stress the importance of the following:

"Allah has created each person for a particular purpose. Only by complying with their natural disposition (*fitrah*), and following the path that is best suited to their make-up, can people fulfill their unique purpose. It is this fulfillment that renders their servitude accomplished!"

If we can truly grasp the meaning of and internalize this truth, we can no longer feel angered, depressed, annoyed, or critical! For we will be cognizant of the reality that each person can only disclose their own natural disposition, regardless of whether their disposition complies with, or contradicts ours! It is as absurd to question another's motives, as it is to question the liver as to why it doesn't pump like the heart!

Indeed, this truth is the essence and the summary of the System and the Order as described by the Quran.

As long as someone fails to comprehend this reality, their claims to believe in a God are false; their faith is only an imitation.

Real faith is the fruit of the comprehension, internalization and the application of this reality.

First of all, a Sufi aspirant **must abandon his anger!** For as soon as one is angered by something, one is veritably dismissing and denying Allah! Each individual can only execute what is in his creation program. To become infuriated by another is no different than being infuriated by the disposition assigned to him by Allah, i.e. **the decree of Allah.**

If Allah has willed to create that individual with that particular program, how can we question His Absolute Knowledge and Will? Clearly, Allah has deliberately chosen to designate that particular composition to that particular individual. To think he or she is wrong, or flawed or inappropriate, is to undermine, doubt and even deny the Godhead of Allah!

Question:

What do dreams signify? Do they have a valid place in the System? How do we see what we see in our dreams, do our spirits leave our body and go elsewhere?

The term **'astral travelling'** denotes a state of the brain, where the emission of a certain kind of radar waves, projects certain images to our brain, allowing us to see and experience certain things or events.

The general conception is that the spirit leaves the body when we sleep, takes a little tour, then re-enters at the time of waking. This isn't so! The spirit does not leave the body or go anywhere! The enlightened ones, who have been able to activate their third eye, have mastered the ability to direct their radar waves to a particular location and perceive that place through images that get projected back to their brains.

Those who are ignorant of the mechanics of this process think their spirits actually leave their body and go to some other place.

Whereas the spirit can only leave the body in two ways:

1. Death

2. Conquest (*fath*)

The truly enlightened ones, who have been able to conquer their souls, who have **'died before death'** and attained the state of *Haqq al-yakeen* (The Certainty of The Reality), are the only ones who can observe without the body. All other observers rely on the radar waves omitted by their brain![17]

The **radar waves** can either be a miracle, based and directed to the material dimensions above **Earth,** or a phenomenon based and directed to the dimensions of **Heaven, Hell** and **the Intermediate Realm.** It can also be directed towards lower dimensions, depending on the expansion capacity of the brain.

To give an example, when we dream of angels, we see them in various forms and figures with which we are already familiar.

---

[17] This topic has been covered in detail in my book *A Guide To Prayer And Dhikr* for those who may be interested.

Angels do not have 'forms' in their original state; they only have certain frequencies in relation to their particular function. In other words, angels are 'high frequency vibrations'. **When one of these frequencies reaches our brain, we crosscheck it with our pre-existing database and decode it based on the closest frequency we can find, and then assign an image to it.**

When a tree talks in our dream for example, it's actually an angel; a high frequency vibration that got decoded and interpreted as a tree as this was the closest frequency the brain was able to find in its database!

As such, when various incoming frequencies reach the brain, an automatic search engine is activated to find the closest corresponding match in order to 'define' it. Whatever form has already been assigned to that closest match remains unchanged. Hence, we see dreams in symbols and not in their original state.

If we take it a step further… **Muhammad (saw)** says:

"People are asleep and will be awakened with death!"

What does this mean? If this life is like sleep, then we must all be dreaming! **This world, and everything in it, is like a dream in respect of the afterlife…** Everything we experience here, the pain, the joy, our possessions, our loved ones… all of it is going to feel like a dream when we wake up to the afterlife with death… And just like we perceive dreams, in the form of symbols as a result of our brain's frequency converting mechanism, so too we perceive everything in this dimension by the very same process.

All of this is confirmed by the world's leading neurophysiologist, Stanford University professor Karl Pribram and the world famous physicist, David Bohm.

Question:

Can people have different perceptions of the same object?

If the same frequency reaches two different people with the same database, then the resulting evaluation will be the same. This is precisely why we all perceive and see the same objects in the same way, because we all have the **same perception mechanism** and have been conditioned to function in pretty much the same way!

The visible spectrum, that is the frequency range that can be detected by the human eye, is definite. Whether the same frequencies reach one eye or 1,000 different eyes, the result will always be the same. They will all see the same thing, as all of them will be processing the incoming data using the same system.

Question:

Why does color blindness result in the different perception of colors?

This is because, in the case of color blindness, there is also a **difference** in the **mechanism of the brain.** That is, a person who is colorblind processes the incoming frequencies differently than a person who isn't. It's not that they receive different frequencies; it's that they possess different brains! The database, i.e., the accumulation of data during one's lifetime, is what defines the brain's capacity.

When we are born, our database consists only of **genetic** and **astrological data**, but as of birth, we are constantly prone to new information, new conditionings, and new data. This is why a newborn baby has limited vision, not because of a lack of sight, but because of the **lack of data** in the brain to 'evaluate' the information.

We can only project outwardly what we possess inwardly. Our ability to decipher a certain input of data depends solely on the database we have been building since our birth.

For example, the tendency to be fond of, and drawn to beauty, is a property of the brain. It may be related to either genetic traits or astrological influences, such as the position of Venus in one's natal chart. In any case, how this inclination externalizes in Iran is different to how it is expressed in Africa, or Japan or the United States of America. Depending on how **environmental conditionings** shapes one's database, traits that are primarily common to the whole of humanity, become externalized through innumerably various means.

Question:

Are 'Heaven' and 'Hell' states of particular frequencies?

All information or 'data' in our database are particular **frequencies.** One's experience of heavenly pleasures is directly proportionate to how rich and comprehensive one's database is. Hence, the different levels of Heaven!

This is why **Muhammad (saw)** encourages the aspiration of knowledge with his words:

"Seek knowledge from the cradle to the grave", for the acquisition of knowledge is what increases the capacity of our database that exists in our brain and gets uploaded to our spirit. Our experience of life is the very result of the information contained in this database. The quality and abundance of knowledge that we supply to it, is what defines our 'experience' of life, and whether it is hell-like or heaven-like.

The Sufis say: *"Abstain from conversing with the foolish!"*

Who are the foolish?

Those who are ignorant of their ignorance!

Why must one 'abstain'? Simply because such people cannot add anything to an aspirant of knowledge. An aspirant should befriend those whose knowledge is greater and further than his, approaching the contrary only with the intent to share his knowledge.

An aspirant seeks to accumulate knowledge with the same eagerness that a worldly person seeks to accumulate money and wealth, as he denies the afterlife. This is because an aspirant knows he cannot attain any more knowledge; hence develop his spirit any more after the point of death. This is why it is crucial for the aspirant to take heed of his masters' words: **"Seek knowledge from cradle to grave", "Seek knowledge even if it is in China", "Befriend those who are ahead of you in knowledge!"**

Commodious knowledge is knowledge that serves useful after death, whereas **useless knowledge serves no purpose in the afterlife.** When the enlightened ones warn us against the attainment of useless knowledge, they are not prohibiting the acquisition of such knowledge altogether but, in fact, advising us not to be fixated or obstructed by it. For all encountered knowledge serves some purpose in life and nothing is encountered by coincidence.

All things experienced by creation are inclusive of their preordained purpose and program. Nothing is without reason. We are all individually equipped with the necessary program to fulfill the purpose the Creator has willed for us. We cannot execute a code that isn't written in our kernel!

Let me give an example from myself...

When I was around the ages of 15-18, I thought of myself as a highly intelligent person. I often wondered why Allah willed for me to be born in Istanbul and not in a more developed country, such as some place in Europe or the USA. I even thought it would have been more befitting if I were born in Mecca or Medina. What was the wisdom behind this will?

After many years, I realized that if I had been born and raised in Mecca or Medina, my religious apprehension would probably not have surpassed the 'literal', disabling me from deciphering the symbolic and metaphoric nature of religion. If I were born in the West, on the other hand, I would probably have become a great scientist, *deprived* however of the knowledge imparted by **Muhammad (saw).**

Allah willed for me to be born in Istanbul instead, a city on the **border of the East and the West,** right in the middle of both worlds! Thus, I was able to benefit both from the teachings of the East and the resources of the West, forming a synthesis of both. I would probably have been deprived of this, had my place of birth on the map been a little more on the left or a little more on the right!

As such, Allah designates the perfect environment and resources required for the fulfillment of every individual's unique purpose.

All of the above is based on a view going **from the Essence to the outer.**

If we employ the counter view, and look at **the Essence from the outer reality**, we may reversely conclude that the people in our lives, our environment, and our occupation are all a herald of either good news or a catastrophe.

When viewed this way interesting things come to mind! One no longer feels the need to say **'I wish…'** for one realizes with conviction that everything is exactly the way it is meant to be and always will be! It is useless to say **'I wish I hadn't done such and such mistake in the past'.** Indeed, that mistake had to be done, those lessons had to be taken, those emotions had to be lived, and everything had to occur in the exact way it did, for us to discover ourselves and accomplish our purposes.

Mistakes and sins teach us valuable lessons. By repenting, we can be cleansed from the sin but the lessons we learn will forever be ours to keep. Life is a journey we must take to reach the destination of our purpose. **Everything that is encountered on this journey including the mistakes we make, is there to aid and guide us in that direction.**

Imagine a staircase of a billion steps. If your purpose in life is to constitute the 22222nd step, then that is exactly where your life experience is going to lead you. Through the people you meet and the events you live, Allah is going to shape you and sculpt you to befit that particular position, not one more or one less.

Allah, in His Pre-Eternal Knowledge, has designed such a magnificent staircase called 'humanity' where each person is preordained to constitute one particular step; no one can escape his role or position in this miraculous staircase.

Sooner or later, each person will play out his role and constitute the step that has been assigned for him. Once the staircase is completed, doomsday will occur.

Although I mentioned the word 'preordained', let us also be aware of the verse:

"Every day He manifests Himself in yet another way."
(Quran 55:29)

That is to say, Allah is present in every dimension, through the various forms within that dimension.

As such, just as it is true that there is no **'free will'** and **only Allah's Will**, it is equally true that every individual lives with his or her own will.

Though they seem to be opposite extremes in contradiction with one another, in fact, they are two sides of the same reality. It's not that there is the greater will of Allah and the lesser will of the people. In its essence, there is no distinction between the two; the distinction arises only by perception. That is, when viewed through the 5 senses, there is dispersion, hence many wills. When viewed through consciousness, there is unity, hence only *One Will.* Consequently, one may claim, "There is a greater will pertaining to Allah" and this will be true, but one may not claim, "There is also a lesser will pertaining to man" or vice versa, as they are different impressions of the *same* thing.

In the realm of consciousness there are no parts or monads, there is only The Whole. What appears to be multiplicity is only the different relations and expressions the Names of the One assume. Hence, when we say 'also' we are denoting 'another' in addition to the One, which is implicative of *shirk* (associating another being with Allah.)

Like the staircase we mentioned of above, if we eliminate one single step from the staircase, would it mean anything on its own? *Together,* the steps form the staircase; they have no substantial existence on their own, as one single step does not lead one anywhere. The Will of the One is like the staircase; the individual steps that compose it are not *separate* or *different* from it. Thus, what we refer to, when we say **'individual will'**, is essentially no different than the ultimate one will. As this staircase continues to evolve and extend, different manifestations appear. The verse, about Allah disclosing Himself in different ways every day, is in reference to these manifestations.

When Allah's attribute of life is reflected on us, we say "I'm alive". Our immortality is in respect of our source of life, being the life attribute of Allah. The same can be said about our knowledge, will, power and so on.

If we can change the direction of our view and start looking at things from the core rather than the outer shell, we may actually realize that everything we manifest is from Allah and submission to this divine guidance will inevitably take us to the actualization of our potentials.

The pre-ordainment, which we have discussed, does not in any way suggest that we sit back and do nothing as everything is already predetermined! The System does not allow inactivity! One who is static cannot survive in the System, just as the primary cell, formed by the sperm and the egg, would not have amounted to anything if it had said, "I have already been preordained to be a human being so there is no need for me to undergo division and proliferation..." Indeed, it is impossible for the cell not to proliferate. It goes against its nature; it can't help but multiply!

In just the same way, we can't help but be ourselves. Whichever step we have been ordained to be, in the staircase of humanity, we will be!

The ultimate destination is contained in the primary cell of our being. That cell contains my characteristics, i.e., by genotype and phenotype but it doesn't define me in every detail.

When we look at things from an astrological view for example, we say that we are currently under the effect of Uranus, where Uranus reflects the traits of Aquarius. This does not mean we can conclude from this that "Hulusi is going to write a book" or "Hulusi is going to contemplate on such and such".

The incoming new **wave** from Uranus will definitely **stimulate certain thought processes, but the results will vary amongst individuals according to their already existing databases.** If my database is ready to output a new thought, then the incoming stimulus will have a favorable effect on my intellect. But if I lack this capacity, or am not in a receiving mode, then the same wave will come to me but have no effect on my brain function. The various planetary influences that reach the brain are nothing more than stimuli to activate certain parts of the brain.

Another example can be given of medical experiments performed on cats. Sexual activity of cats was observed to increase significantly when the sex centers in their brains were stimulated with electrodes. When their anger centers were stimulated, they started to growl. Thus it can be understood that when certain sections of the brain are 'irritated' the brain responds. Likewise, when astrological data reach the brain it comes in an elementary format, without a particular notion. Depending on which part of the brain receives the data, how it processes it, the contents of its database, and the interpretation it makes, the resulting behaviors differ.

As for fate...

A final destination and a general path to lead us there, have been predetermined for us. Everything else depends on the individual program we run, and its natural consequences. Our program is constantly in synch with the angelic influences coming from our dimensional depths. Hence, our behavior is a synthesis of both the inward, and the outward influences that constantly surround us.

This formation is what we call the **'individual will'**. To deny the individual will is to deny this formation! To say that the individual will and the 'Will of the One' are 'one and the same thing', is not to deny the individual will; just as claiming ice to be water doesn't negate the formation called 'ice' (but doesn't assign a *separate* existence to ice either.)

When we observe the reality from the dimension of pure consciousness, we cannot see anything in existence other than the One. In this state, there is no dispersion or multitude; there is no 'other' to possess a separate will. Only when we observe from an individual point of view, that is the dimension of multiplicity, we see individualized expressions of the One Will, which appear to be many, but, in essence, they come from the same source.

The Quran elucidates this matter to those of understanding by saying **"You will only live the consequences of your own actions"**, referring to the individual will in the domain of multiplicity. Then, reflecting it from the projection of unity, it says **"There is only one** will: **Allah"**, referring to the reality that **"there is no existence other than Allah."**

Both are true, as both are different projections of the same reality.

Note that the verse says **"Everyday He manifests Himself in yet another way"**; it does not say **'Allah'**. He is translated from the Arabic word **'*HU*'**, which does not connote gender, of course, but connotes a pure being beyond description.

We can think of *HU* as the dimension of unity in the essence of each monad, the source of the constant formation.

***HU* is the unity disguised as multiplicity. *HU* is the dimension of oneness implicit in the essence of all things!**

Question:

Is the acquisition of knowledge in our control? How does it affect our future; the 'step' we have been destined to compose?

Knowledge, experience and guidance shape us into becoming the 'step' we are meant to be. The degree, to which someone acquires and applies knowledge, is the degree of 'shaping' that occurs. Without getting shaped, one cannot become. Therefore, knowledge without application is futile.

Let's say, for example, that I have attained much knowledge and internalized the fact that each individual can only express his, or her, natural disposition and can't display behavior beyond the limits of his capacity. Now let's suppose I go to a restaurant, the waiter comes and throws the menu at me. Can I get angry or yell at him? He is only displaying the behavior resulting from his internal program; obviously he lacks the data to enable him to act in a different way!

If I were ignorant of this truth, I would react with anger and frustration. I would question his behavior with fury and try to correct him. Knowledge enables me to remain calm, to not react with emotions. Knowledge saves me from the unnecessary burdens of impulsive reactions and the tiresome repercussions arising as a result.

When a person gets infuriated and angry, millions of cells are terminated instantly! One moment of anger, depending on its intensity, can cause millions of short circuits and explosions at the molecular level, sometimes even damaging irreplaceable brain cells! So how can a learned person who has acquired knowledge display such behavior and cause his own demise? Could this be true knowledge? If knowledge does not prevent us from harming ourselves and others, if knowledge does not 'shape' us, then we cannot really claim to have knowledge.

The cut of a diamond is what determines its value. A one-carat diamond, with 52 facets, is much more valuable than the same diamond with 32 facets, or 16 facets. **The more a diamond is cut, the more its value will increase.**

We, also, are like diamonds. The more knowledge cuts and shapes us, the more we increase in value.

Question:

If the level of knowledge that I can acquire is up to me, that is, if I'm in charge of using my brain to evaluate knowledge, then it's logical to assume that the 'step' we form in the staircase is not fixed, which means the staircase itself is not stable?

Our place in the staircase is fixed. The place we occupy, the 'step' we compose is the very purpose of our creation. However, its final shape is determined at the point of death. So long as we are living, we are still being cut and shaped.

As for the 'shaping' that happens in hell, it is like a final cleansing of the residues of impurities we carry from our worldly life. Like purifying gold with fire, it doesn't add any further value to it; only purifies it.

As such, **hell is not a place of getting shaped, but rather, it is a place of purification.**

Hellfire purifies and solidifies the things we've gained in the world, so that we may enter heaven as refined beings.

No matter what the apparent reason may be, everyone experiences an intermediate phase in their lives, during which they suffer an internal burning. This burning, referred to as 'hellfire', is a way of cleansing ourselves from inappropriate states that impede our heavenly existence.

Those, who are destined to stay in hell forever, will also eventually reach a state of refinement after intense and extended suffering.

But at the end of all suffering, the fire will be extinguished, the burning will end, and **new life will spring from the ashes.**

ABOUT THE AUTHOR

Ahmed Hulusi (Born January 21, 1945, Istanbul, Turkey) contemporary Islamic philosopher. From 1965 to this day he has written close to 30 books. His books are written based on Sufi wisdom and explain Islam through scientific principles. His established belief that the knowledge of Allah can only be properly shared without any expectation of return has led him to offer all of his works which include books, articles, and videos free of charge via his web-site. In 1970 he started examining the art of spirit evocation and linked these subjects parallel references in the Quran (smokeless flames and flames instilling pores). He found that these references were in fact pointing to luminous energy which led him to write *Spirit, Man, Jinn* while working as a journalist for the Aksam newspaper in Turkey. Published in 1985, his work called *Mysteries of Man (Insan ve Sirlari)* was Hulusi's first foray into decoding the messages of the Quran filled with metaphors and examples through a scientific backdrop. In 1991 he published *A Guide To Prayer And Dhikr (Dua and Zikir)* where he explains how the repetition of certain prayers and words can lead to the realization of the divine attributes inherent within our essence through increased brain capacity. In 2009 he completed his final work, *The Key to the Quran through reflections of the Knowledge of Allah* which encompasses the understanding of leading Sufi scholars such as Abdulkarim al Jili, Abdul-Qadir Gilani, Muhyiddin Ibn al-Arabi, Imam Rabbani, Ahmed ar-Rifai, Imam Ghazali, and Razi, and which approached the messages of the Quran through the secret Key of the letter 'B'.